I0487949

Taming the Dragons

Taming the Dragons

50 Essays from the Business World

Paula Gamonal

Writers Club Press

San Jose New York Lincoln Shanghai

Taming the Dragons
50 Essays from the Business World

All Rights Reserved © 2001 by Ravenwerks

No part of this book may be reproduced or transmitted in any form or by any means, graphic, electronic, or mechanical, including photocopying, recording, taping, or by any information storage retrieval system, without the permission in writing from the publisher.

Writers Club Press
an imprint of iUniverse.com, Inc.

For information address:
iUniverse.com, Inc.
5220 S 16th, Ste. 200
Lincoln, NE 68512
www.iuniverse.com

Cover Photography by Thomas Photography, Tooele, Utah

ISBN: 0-595-19512-1

Printed in the United States of America

This book is dedicated to everyone who enjoyed these essays in their original versions in the Ravenwerks Newsletter and honored us by requesting that they be reprinted in a more permanent form.

It is also dedicated to anyone who feels that business is an arena to improve the lives of the people they serve, including customers, clients, and co-workers.

EPIGRAPH

Life shrinks or expands in proportion to one's courage.

-Anaïs Nin

CONTENTS

PREFACE

Where did the idea for the book originate?

The Ravenwerks Information Center web site has found itself the focal point for a community of business executives and managers-we've been exchanging ideas on business and people management for a few years. Our readers comment on articles, suggest ideas, and participate in questions and answers in a newsletter. We've had lots of people signing their bosses up for our newsletter, or anonymously putting copies on co-workers' desks. We thought, "this is something that people really need to know and have an interest in!"

Why publish this as a book, since most of your material is on the Web?

People wanted it in a format that was more comfortable to read and refer to later-rather than asking about an article they thought they remembered from a few months ago in one of our newsletters. They also wanted to be able to give it as a gift. One professional coach we know wanted to use it as required reading for all of the folks that she coaches. It's difficult to do that with online material. It's also easier to read on the bus or in the bathtub.

Who should read this book?

Ask any manager what his most frustrating problem is, and he will probably tell you "People." The things that prevent a good manager from being an excellent one are usually "people" skills-being able to sell an important client on a good idea, or resolve a conflict between two strong-minded employees, or improve communications between two departments that are "silos."

This book is for anyone who manages people in any business-whether they're students of management or experienced managers of companies with several divisions. From the readers of our web sites and discussion groups, we've learned that the problems faced at any level are surprisingly similar. People are people. If you can learn how to manage them, you'll be successful, regardless of the industry you're in or the level you're starting at.

How is this different from all the other business management titles in the bookstores?

In the bookstores, you'll find titles on what we call the "flavor of the week" in business management styles. Business management science, project management methodologies, cross-functional teams, Quality Improvement, political correctness, and a thousand other things. You can spend your life reading business books.

This book was designed for the style of busy managers. You don't have to read the whole book to find something useful and effective that you can use right away. You can open the book anywhere, read an essay in five or ten minutes and usually find a concrete way to apply it in your own business that will give you immediate results.

What is the biggest problem in business?

99% of the problems in business happen because people don't communicate. The average employee that is seen as "nonproductive" can be turned into a star employee by a manager who spends a very little time and effort figuring out where he's coming from, finding a way to make a connection, and providing the motivation, information and tools that employee needs to become a major contributor to the company's success.

Most companies know that communication is a huge issue, but they haven't a clue how to address it, so they throw money at the problem to publish a newsletter or develop an intranet. The problem is that it becomes a "fluff bucket" of superficial data that isn't really useful to the employee.

There are very simple but very effective ways to figure out what's needed and provide them inexpensively.

ACKNOWLEDGEMENTS

I would like to thank the subscribers of Ravenwerks who sent insightful comments and ideas, which became the fodder for these essays.

I am grateful to the people who taught me that being an ethical human being could actually enhance your ability to survive in Corporate America, as strange as it may sound.

My parents.

Rick Mead, a senior manager who listened to all of my crazy ideas and let me try some of them.

Dennis Astin, technology project manager who puts his family miles above business and is still one of the most dedicated businesspeople I know.

Debby Sills, Beth Wodzinski, Jenny Hollingshead, Marnie Ellison, Matt Herrmann, Jenny Jessop, Stan Uno, Julie Jacobs and all the others who have called me manager or coach at one time or another and taught me a thousand times more than I could have ever taught any of them.

Most of all, I would like to thank John Williams, senior executive, consulting engagement manager, technology project manager and mentor who makes it all look like fun.

INTRODUCTION

The imagery of dragons is a vivid and compelling metaphor for the dynamics of people in the corporate world. Dragons are a paradox-something dangerous and powerful-courted by some, avoided by others, but ignored by no one.

The Western paradigm is exemplified by some of the oldest pieces of literature in the Romance languages-the myth of St. George and the epic poem of Beowulf.

St. George rescued a Libyan king's daughter from an evil dragon. In return for the dragon's head, the king promised that all of his subjects would be baptized as Christians. St. George is revered as an icon of martial valor and selflessness in the Christian world, and became the patron saint of England.

The oldest known piece of literature in the English language is the epic poem Beowulf. At the end of the poem, the heroic king's last act of valor was to kill a dragon, with the help of his bravest warrior, Wiglaf. Beowulf won the encounter with the fire-breathing, poisonous serpent. He later died of his wounds, comforted by the knowledge that the dragon's hoarded gold would support his kingdom in times of famine.

The Western paradigm of dragons parallels the attitude of many people in the corporate culture toward politics, change, and other perils of business and economy.

Fear manifests itself in either avoidance or combat. Avoidance by attempting to "stay out" of water-cooler politics, laying low and hoping not to be noticed for the next round of layoffs. Combat by engaging in fierce competition over positions or market share.

In Eastern art and literature, the dragon looks remarkably similar—it's still a huge, reptilian creature with claws, fangs and wings—but it is seen as a beautiful symbol of abundance and blessing.

In Chinese mythology, Eastern dragons are benevolent, helpful and wise.

Chinese people around the world call themselves "Lung Tik Chuan Ren" or Descendents of the Dragon. Both male and female dragons have mated with humans in mythology and their descendants have been powerful rulers. The Japanese emperor Hirohito traced his ancestry back 125 generations to the daughter of the Dragon King of the Sea.

Eastern dragons fill a role similar to angels in the Western culture—in that they are worshipped and revered as protectors. Pagodas, temples and shrines throughout China allow supplicants to burn incense and pray to dragons. The Black Dragon Pool Chapel, near Peking, was reserved for the Empress and her court.

Rather than being poisonous, dragons are thought to give life. The dragon's breath is called "sheng chi" or divine energy.

Superimposed on the corporate world, this view supplies an alternative-observing the natural rhythms of the market and the economy. Appreciating and engaging the personal characteristics of people that we work with or compete against.

The apparent paradox between the Eastern and Western view of dragons is a fantastic illustration of how business people react to the unpredictable and often chaotic forces that steer businesses and careers toward failure or success. Looking at the same situation, one person sees danger where another sees opportunity.

The corporate world has always been full of dragons. How you deal with them (and how they deal with YOU) often depends more on your point of view than on the weapons you hold.

1. On Changing the Rules

We started trying to set up a small anarchist community, but the people wouldn't obey the rules.

-Alan Bennett

Integrity has no need of rules.

-Albert Camus

You've heard the proverb-"It's not whether you win or lose, but how you play the game." Sometimes, knowing when to CHANGE the game is perhaps more important than winning or losing.

Note: This is NOT about lying, cheating and stealing, although I suppose understanding this concept would make you more successful, even at that.

This is about focusing on the objective, rather than the means. To use a tennis metaphor, this means concentrating on the seams and yellow fuzz on the ball, rather than focusing on your grip on the racket.

A friend of mine told me about an experience in an MBA class. One of his professors (who had 26 students) handed out one red card to each student.

The professor held 26 black cards. Each unmatched card was worth nothing, but each red/black card combination was worth $100. (To be paid by the dean at the conclusion of the game.) The students, at first, thought the game to be a fairly simple one-they would either sell their red cards to the professor for $50, or would buy a black card from the professor for $50.

The dean would pay out a total of $2600. How that would be divided depended on how each party played the game. Since the professor needed the red cards to make a profit this seemed a pretty easy bet.

1

However, the professor, in a public display, burned three of his black cards. This meant that at least three of the students' red cards were now worthless. The students were faced with a much more interesting dilemma-their options:

- Sell their cards for less than $50, (since they would be lucky to get any profit from the game at this point.)
- Or they could organize and leverage their communal power to force the professor's hand.

There were other options that were not as obvious, if they used enough creativity. It's possible (I don't know whether the dean would approve) that they could manufacture more black cards. This brought in the whole ethical argument about whether or not that was "fair," but since it wasn't explicitly stated that they couldn't, and since the professor had set a pretty creative example himself by burning three black cards. . .

I don't know how the game ended (maybe it's still going on!) But the point was fairly clear-you don't always have to play the game as the "rules" appear on the surface.

Don't assume you have to play the same game everyone else is playing. If you look carefully at the underlying dynamics, you may find the difference between the ultimate objective and the means people typically use to reach that objective. You can stay within your philosophy and your ethics and still change the rules of the game you're playing to your advantage. (And to the advantage of your co-workers, clients, and company!)

2. ON CREATIVITY

When we lose the right to be different, we lose the privilege to be free.
-Charles Evans Hughes

Removing the faults in a stage-coach may produce a perfect stage-coach, but it is unlikely to produce the first motor car.
-Edward De Bono

The secret to creativity is knowing how to hide your sources.
-Albert Einstein

If you want to make enemies, try to change something.
-Woodrow Wilson

Genius....means little more than the faculty of perceiving in an unhabitual way.
-William James

It has been argued that the greatest strength the United States has in the world economy is the creativity of our people, fostered by the market economy that rewards innovation. That spirit of innovation is now being taken a step further by technology. Our children are growing up with computers as tools to help give light, color and sound to the fantastic things in their heads. It takes less time and money to communicate creative thoughts in rich, colorful, animated ways. It is not uncommon for a fourth-grade book report to be a professional-looking animated multimedia presentation on "The World of Bats."

There are challenges to maintaining your personal, innate creativity in the pressures of the business world. There are also challenges to leading and managing creative people so that they can exercise their talents in ways that are the most likely to find their way to the bottom line of your company.

Personal Creativity

With a schedule full of appointments and a head full of day-to-day problems to solve, it seems the higher one climbs up the corporate ladder the less compatible the day to day world is with the creative process. One of the very most important things a business leader can do, however, is to have a vivid long-range vision, (and probably several shorter-range visions) and to be able to communicate that vision to others.

Developing that long-range vision, as well as finding compelling ways to communicate it to employees, clients, vendors and other parties, takes a lot of creativity. Where do you find it? Here are some ways to get your creativity jumpstarted:

- Allow yourself time and space. In his book "How to become CEO," Jeffrey J. Fox recommends that you carve out an hour of "do-not-disturb" time into your schedule EVERY DAY and to use that time thinking. The discipline of setting aside that time will make it easier for you to "shift gears" from critical thinking, which is where most business people spend most of their time; to creative thinking.

- Separate the creative process from the critical process. Both are vital, but many managers become more accustomed to critical thinking-they receive plans and strategies from their subordinates and spend most of their time fine-tuning and critiquing them. Many people also spend an inordinate amount of time critiquing themselves and their own ideas. They come up with a great idea, but before the idea gets fully fleshed out, it becomes the victim of a hundred negative thoughts-pragmatic concerns, doubts, fears, conflicts with other priorities, etc. Instead of letting the critical process take precedence, try this-when you come up with a great idea, give it the time and space to develop itself fully. Write or draw it out and let it sit for a day before attacking it with critical thoughts.

- Concentrate on the long-range vision or "future state" of what you want your company to look like in three to five years, rather than the steps of getting from here to there. Don't worry about the "how you're going to get there" until you fully understand and can clearly communication "where we're going." If you can describe an ideal "future state" clearly enough, the steps and the process of getting there tend to become much easier than you'd originally thought.

- Respect your "muse" and always be ready when inspiration strikes. Always carry a pen and paper (or a palm or laptop computer, or whatever you're comfortable with.) I carry a planner with several colored pens because I find it easier to describe and classify thoughts using color so that I'll be able to understand them later, when I have time to review my notes and develop ideas more fully. Inspiration may strike while waiting in line, in a meeting on another topic, at lunch with friends, or while traveling. Never let a good idea escape. Cast a net of words or drawings around it so that you can remember it later.

- Many people find that inspiration strikes first thing in the morning, or even in the middle of the night. If this is the case for you, make appropriate accommodations. This is not to say you should stay up all night working on presentations, but keep a notebook by your bed for quick sketches, words or outlines. Then relax and go back to sleep. Most likely your "triggers" will help you remember your idea in the morning.

- Use methods that work for you. The "Circle Tree" is a method for developing an idea that can be used with equal success, whether employed by yourself on the back of an envelope in twenty minutes on an airplane, or in a creative session with twelve people for four hours.

Team Creativity

Taking the principles of creativity a step further has greater challenges, and greater potential rewards.

Complex objectives usually require the creative energies of more than one person. You may need diverse frames of reference, or diverse skill sets, or diverse experiences. James Watson, who won a Nobel prize with Francis Crick for the discovery of the double helix structure of the DNA, put it simply: "Nothing new that is really interesting comes about without collaboration." The challenge is that creativity requires trust. Unfortunately, the more different you are from someone else, the more difficult it can be to trust him or her.

Most of the projects I've been involved in have required the creative energies of brilliant programmers and equally brilliant business people. Trust between groups of people who are strong-minded and from very different backgrounds is hard to come by, but it often comes from a shared objective—the knowledge that it's in the best interest of both the programmers and the business people to meet or exceed the customers' expectations.

Focusing on external objectives, rather than the relative merits or importance of a particular mode of thinking, gives everyone a common frame of reference. That way, the egos of both groups (and most brilliant people have substantial egos!) are helping, rather than hindering, the process.

If you give an objective to a cross-functional team to work on, be very specific about the vision of the results you're expecting, but don't be too particular about the means they use to accomplish those results. For example, Jon R. Katzenbach and Douglas R. Smith describe an effort in *The Wisdom of Teams* by a team of seven at Burlington Northern in 1981. The challenge was to find ways to adapt to meet changing transportation needs. They did this by improving Burlington's approach to intermodal transportation, (using flatbed train cars to carry truck trailers full of cargo.) Intermodal transportation was viewed by Burlington's power structure at the time as a necessary evil rather than an accepted or embraced way of doing business.

By shifting the paradigm, this team of seven was able to demonstrate the speed, flexibility and efficiency of a new way of doing business. They resoundingly accomplished their objective, but not in the way Burlington had expected it.

A simpler example could involve an objective for a child. A friend of mine told her son that she expected his math grade to improve by the next report card. She expected him to come up with a plan to accomplish that objective and implement it himself. She suggested that he enter a tutoring program at her expense.

The boy approached her with an advertisement for a "slightly educational" computer game. The game was one he had wanted for some time, and only marginally relevant to the skill he has missing, so at first my friend resisted.

Mark explained that the cost of the game was less than that of the tutor. He suggested she buy it, and if he did not get at least a B+ on his next report card, he would repay her out of his allowance. My friend took the "bet," Mark's grades improved, he kept his allowance, and everybody won. By giving Mark a margin of latitude and trust, she got his own motives involved and gave him a greater stake in an effective outcome. Whether Mark's grades improved because of the computer game or because of his motivation to win the bet (or a combination of the two) is irrelevant. Both parties achieved what they wanted by linking their motives and engaging their resources.

Most businesses are more conducive to critical thinking than creative thinking. By respecting your own and your coworkers' creativity enough to give it the time, space and tools it needs, you give yourself and your organizations a powerful advantage.

3. ON FEAR

You gain strength, courage, and confidence by every experience in which you stop to look fear in the face.

-Eleanor Roosevelt

Fear is a darkroom where negatives develop.

-Usman Asif

Fear is debilitating to the person afflicted with it. Fear is also repellent to the people you spend time with. Managers are reluctant to trust people who exhibit symptoms of nervousness or fear, because fearful people are more likely to make mistakes. They are mentally and physically restricted and/or reactive. Customers and clients avoid fearful people for the same reasons.

We typically act as though stress is a problem of the modern age. We live in an age of corporate acquisitions, layoffs, rising interest, fluctuating stock prices, energy crises and gang violence. The usage of the word "stress" is relatively new, (past 20 years or so) but there has always been fear.

Although our ancestors probably didn't worry about their cholesterol levels or the depletion of the ozone layer, they were probably more afraid than we are today of being attacked by wild animals or contracting dysentery. In a way, this euphemizing and reluctance to confront and deal with fear is unfortunate, because real, concrete fears are easier to identify and to do something about than this nebulous "stress" that seems to surround people and organizations today.

Learning to recognize fear, distancing yourself from the source, and THEN addressing the cause makes you a much more powerful person in the face of the stresses that the corporate culture is so good at dishing out.

Recognizing Fear

The first step is to understand that fear is debilitating, and to commit to dealing with it early when you see it in yourself. Besides all of the very real, documented health risks associated with stress, there are also less easily quantifiable damages.

When we are afraid, we tighten up our physical and mental processes – just when we need them most to meet whatever lurking challenge is causing the fear.

In the new Star Wars Episode I, Yoda (one of the wisest characters in popular "literature") said to Anakin Skywalker-"There is fear in you. Fear leads to anger. Anger leads to hatred. Hatred leads to the Dark Side." This is a metaphorical example of a very real series of reactions that can be arrested if we catch it early and deal with the source of our fear.

The most important thing is to learn your own symptoms. A friend of mine noticed that her left hand goes numb when she's stressed or fearful. (She has no idea why this happens physiologically, we assume it has something to do with posture and tightening muscles that are restricting blood flow in some way-but that's beside the point.) Another coworker gets headaches. Grinding teeth, clenching back or shoulder muscles, and having stomach problems are all common physical symptoms of stress. Learn to recognize yours and take immediate action.

Distancing Yourself From the Source

When my eleven-year-old son begins to get uneasy in a movie, he looks for the exit signs. This helps him put some emotional distance between himself and the situation that is causing fear. Then it becomes HIS decision.

He's in control of a scale, with his fear of the monsters on the screen on one side of the scale, and his reasons for staying on the other. "I paid good allowance money to be here, I want to find out what happens, and I want to be with my friends." If the scale tips too far the other way, he can always leave, but he's never actually had to.

Building some time and space between yourself and the source of your fear gives you a "safe place" to exercise your mental and creative skills. It's much easier to be brilliant and creative when you're not paralyzed with fear or knocking your knees together.

John Williams, a former helicopter pilot in the Air Force calls this "compartmentalization." He says it was part of his training as a pilot. Compartmentalization involves sealing off the fear into a compartment of your brain so that it doesn't affect your ability to sense and react to the needs of the situation. This is vital to the survival of someone in a combat situation. Although most situations aren't quite that extreme, I can see how it's a useful skill.

Here's a more "down to earth" tactic for those of us who don't fly helicopters in combat: one of the simplest ways to put some distance between yourself and your fears is to make sure you have adequate insurance and a financial safety cushion (that is kept in a secure but liquid form!) There are plenty of books on the topic of financial security that explain this much better than we could here.

Humor is also great distance-builder. Especially when a group of people is in a tense situation, a healthy dose of laughter will help put things in perspective. A very good project manager I know insists during interviews that he will not hire anyone that cannot laugh and have a good time, even (and especially) during a crisis. Being able to laugh at yourself for being so paranoid will release some of the pressure you're feeling.

Another good way to distance yourself from the source of your fear is to cultivate diverse skills and aptitudes. If you're a programmer, learn creative writing or management skills. If you work in the health industry, learn something about the finance industry. This diversity will add depth to your "day job" by giving you another frame of reference, and will also give you greater stability in a changing world.

When most of us are under stress, we abuse ourselves more. We work late hours and don't have time to eat right, exercise, recreate and meditate. Unfortunately, this is when we most need our physical capacities to be at their best. If you don't plan the time to take care of yourself, your body might mutiny and impose relaxation because of illness. Plan the time to exercise, enjoy healthy meals, take your vitamins, play with your kids, attend church or meditate if you choose. Whatever you normally do that makes you feel good should become even more of a priority.

Many people need to write or talk. This "brain-dumping" is a good way to force the problem through the verbal process-to make it take a tangible form that is separate from us and can then be scrutinized and dissected. Problems are seldom as bad as they seem, especially if we can get them on paper where we can see them objectively. This doesn't have to be pretty or organized, especially for the first pass.

We also tend to abuse or neglect our relationships when we're fearful. Besides being in a time crunch, many of us feel that our family and friends "have enough problems of their own." We want to protect them from worry and maybe tell them later after "everything has been ironed out." This is a tough call, because we obviously want to protect those we love. But in many cases, they can tell something is wrong and keeping the reasons from them will only make them more fearful, since they are guessing at the cause and feeling left out.

A friend of mine takes long walks with his wife when he's going through particularly stressful times on his projects. This does a number of good things-it helps him verbalize the situations, get a neutral perspective, strengthen his relationship, and get some exercise at the same time.

During a particularly stressful time, my friend and his wife lost track of how far they'd walked and ended up calling their teenaged son to bring the car and pick them up! I'm sure that brought some chuckles, but probably did them all some good.

Addressing the Cause

Once you've recognized the symptoms of fear and distanced yourself from the cause, it is much easier to figure out a way to resolve it appropriately without overreacting or being in denial.

From this "safe bubble" of time and space that you've created for yourself, objectively evaluate the worst possible outcome. This is usually not death or dismemberment, but could involve some serious setbacks. Once you have accepted the thought of the worst possibility, it's much easier to improve upon that without trepidation.

Evaluate the source of your fear and exercise the creative and mental processes you use best. If you're a creative thinker, visualize your way out of the problem with markers on a whiteboard. If you're a linear thinker, string it out into a Gantt chart. If you're a writer, write it out.

Most people are much more comfortable with a tangible plan of action than with a messy nebulae of anxiety.

Learning to recognize and acknowledge the first physical signs of fear in yourself allows you to take action before any of the possible negative effects can set in. Immediately isolate yourself to create time and space to work in, and address the cause directly. If you can do this effectively every time, tell me how. If you can do it effectively some of the time, you've gained a huge advantage, not only in your chances for personal and professional success, but for the quality of your life as well.

4. ON CHANGE

Change is the only true constant.

-Unknown

A ship in harbor is safe, but that's not what ships are built for

-John A. Shedd

It is only the wisest and the stupidest that cannot change.

-Confucius Analects

Absolutely improbable things happen in real life as well as weak literature.

-Ada Leverson

A very bright young lady that I'm coaching is finding out about the realities of change in the workplace the hard way.

Amy (not her real name) just finished a glowingly successful project. She built a high-performance team from the ground up. They learned the ropes of the project, established processes, explored one another's strengths and found new ones, and built up trust in one another's performance. They won accolades, individually and as a team, for their brilliant performance.

They were so successful that they quickly completed the project and worked themselves into obsolescence.

Now what? They could, probably legitimately, stretch out the process of "tying up loose ends" and prolong their togetherness; or they could disband and find new positions and projects and start over from scratch.

The more successful people are, the more change they will probably be subjected to in their careers.

It didn't used to be that way. Success used to mean having a secure position, moving predictably up the corporate ladder of a single company for the entire length of a career, concentrating on a single business or industry (or even a single product!)

Nowadays, however, success brings change. Even if you stay with the same company, you have to adapt constantly to stay abreast of a changing marketplace. You need to adapt to new people, new technology, and new ways of doing things.

Rather than a ladder of success, it's more of a spiral that twists and turns unpredictably and sometimes disturbingly.

Amy bravely, and wisely, chose to launch herself wholeheartedly into a new project in a different part of the company. She will struggle for a while. It's hard to give up a team and project that supplies a great deal of satisfaction-both professionally and socially; to face a pile of unknowns with a group of people who aren't sure they even like one another, much less trust each other with their chances for professional success.

In his Seven Habits for Highly Effective People, Steven Covey describes one of the habits as "beginning with the end in mind," which means you have to picture your goal with great detail and clarity, but not be too rigid about the path between here and there. It may take some turns you're not expecting. Most airline flights deviate a certain percentage off the planned flight path, but passengers have a high degree of confidence that when they get on a plane bound for New York, they'll end up in New York, despite turbulence, storms, traffic, and other anomalies.

Amy knows, even in the middle of all this, that her best chance for success involves going beyond the familiar and comfortable. The opportunity for success with her last project team had been met and exploited. Any further work with that group would have been anticlimactic, and delaying its end would have compromised the hard-won reputation she had for getting things done on time and on schedule.

It might take months, or even years, to bring her new team to those levels of trust and performance. But that's what she's good at. She'll be fine and she knows it.

5. ON PATIENCE

God, grant me patience. And I need it right now!

-Unknown

In these days of 27-year-old Internet billionaires, it's hard to make a case for the virtue of patience. The icons of success that you see on the covers of magazines and hear about on the news are those that are first and fastest.

What we forget is that there are, and have always been, get-rich-quick schemes, and there have always been a few poster children for each "boom."

Just from US History, there was the prospect of gold in the New World, land rushes, gold rushes, stock market miracles, and industrial conglomerations. For every glowing success from these situations, there are thousands more who lost quickly.

I've received hundreds of pieces of e-mail (have no clue how I got on all these lists) in the last six months offering to make me rich overnight. Gambling is gambling-I have nothing against putting a quarter in a slot machine for recreation, but I don't want to do business and base my family's security on a gamble.

I keep reminding myself that anything worth doing is worth taking the time.

In raising a child, gardening, making dinner, or running a business, I firmly believe that you ALWAYS get better results if you take your time and don't cut corners. Business is dealing with people. It's a natural process, same as any of the other activities I mentioned. Taking your time does a lot of good:

- It allows information to shift from short to long-term memory.

- It allows you to obtain information from a wider variety of sources.

- You can view situations from a broader perspective.
- Other people have time to internalize your ideas and get "on board," rather than merely taking orders.
- You have time to produce high quality work.

Using planning tools helps you to keep tabs on things without breathing down people's necks. We list tasks that we know we need to get to a specific result, and then string those tasks out chronologically.

Which need to be done first? Which are dependent on each other (or on something external?) Once the plan is done, sit back and let it happen! There will be times when more effort is required, but during times when your involvement isn't required, devote your energy to something else rather than fussing over the outcome.

When I was a child, my grandfather (an excellent gardener) gave me a potted plant of my own to take care of. I was thrilled with the little plant, and wanted it to grow faster. I watered it every day. Needless to say, it died. (Probably from drowning!)

My grandfather, being a very wise man, then gave me an entire garden plot. There was enough work to do weeding and watering and fussing over 20 or so plants that they were much safer from my well-meaning but overly enthusiastic attentions.

For some of the same reasons, Jeffrey Fox recommends taking vacations in his book *"How to Become CEO."* Taking vacations gives you a chance to put things into perspective, devote your energy to something different from what you do for a living every day, and evaluate the differences when you come back.

Having a hobby that's as different as possible from your primary occupation is also a good thing. It causes you to "change gears" and use and develop different skills and experiences from those you normally would. You'd be surprised at how bringing a different perspective to the same job will allow you to see it differently. That is why people with longer, more liberal and diversified education tend to be more successful in the long run than people with specific, short term education like technical certificates.

The last point I would ask you to consider is patience with other people. People have different motives, rhythms and work styles.

I have often struggled with individuals who seem to speak so slowly that it is really an effort not to finish their sentences for them. Besides being rude, this is disconcerting to them and undermines their effectiveness.

I've since learned to take a deep breath and try to adjust my rhythm to theirs. It's a refreshing break from the action-oriented running around that the corporate culture pushes us toward. I find myself thinking more deeply and creatively after talking with a person like that.

Even when the world is moving faster than the speed of a T1 Internet access line, patience is, was and always will be a virtue that is sure to add to your personal and organizational success, as long as you don't expect it overnight!

6. ON COMPANY NEWSLETTERS

The worst thing about the miracle of modern communications is the Pavlovian pressure it places upon everyone to communicate whenever a bell rings.

—Russell Baker

Every improvement in communication makes the bore more terrible.
-Frank Moore Colby

The more elaborate our means of communication, the less we communicate.

-Joseph Priestley

Most people don't read their company newsletters. Most consist of birthdays this month, a listing of new babies and anniversaries, what charity event has been sponsored by the management, and a contest for the new color scheme for the bathrooms.

I have nothing against newsletters, per se (obviously, because I've written a lot of them!) but they have to be part of a global, company wide commitment to communications; rather than serving as an excuse for a company's complete internal communication strategy.

People who write fluffy newsletters, by and large, are people with time on their hands. Generally, they have time on their hands because they are 'out of the loop' of what's really going on. The people who should be writing the newsletters are the people in the company with the least time to be doing it.

This is a paradox induced by the lack of emphasis placed on communication by most companies. This contributes to the fluffy newsletters, which further degrades the status of communication in the minds of the stakeholders. This further entrenches the tradition of fluffy newsletters, which in turn get fluffier!

Meanwhile, work is getting duplicated, policies are being ignored, measurements are not being made or are going unnoticed, and employees are clueless about how what they're doing contributes (or detracts from) to the bottom line of the company.

Good communication includes two elements. In the fluffy newsletter scenario, the writer/editor is typically out of touch with one or both of these elements: the audience, or the purpose.

The Audience

What is your workforce like? Are they traditional workers that sit in cubicles in a single location? Are they geographically spread out? Do they work different shifts? Do they work from home? Are there places in your business where they tend to congregate? Does information flow easily up, down and sideways in your company? Are there any departments that seem isolated?

Taking all of this into account will help you develop a list of appropriate communications vehicles that might include:

- Posters, especially including graphs and visuals
- Memos (distribute them on colored or different-sized paper to make them stand out in a full in-box.)
- E-mail
- Intranet
- Conference calls or voice mails
- An open door policy and a genuine appreciation on the part of management for employees who care enough to share information or concerns

- Town-hall type meetings
- A news-stand type table with brochures, newspaper clippings, etc. for employees to browse

If something merits the time and attention to communicate it, make sure you do it thoroughly so nobody gets left out. Use two or more vehicles for anything important. (Note-you shouldn't be communicating anything that isn't important!)

The Purpose

Things that should be communicated to your workforce on a regular basis:

- Company mission, goals and concrete objectives
- Performance measures (stock price, earnings per share, profits, etc.) especially with specifics of how the employees contribute (or could contribute) to improving those measures
- Policy implementations or changes
- Process or workflow changes
- New tools or resources available
- Lessons learned from challenges overcome
- Kudos to any employee or team member for any reason
- Industry or market information

Remember that positive information should get the largest possible interested audience, negative information (particularly performance or disciplinary actions) should be discussed/resolved with the smallest number of people possible.

Give your people the opportunity to contribute to the success of your company by having a thorough, grounded understanding of what your company is about. Most companies seriously underestimate what their people are capable of, given information and an environment that encourages communication.

Newsletters are not bad. But leaving the communications of your company to *just* a newsletter, especially if that newsletter is not something that the management invests time and attention in, is a disservice to your employees. It's also an indication of a company that is not taking full advantage of its best resource-an informed, motivated workforce.

7. ON RESPECT

Never esteem men on account of their riches or their station. Respect goodness, find it where you may.

-William Cobbett

Men are respectable only as they respect.

-Ralph Waldo Emerson

We all agree wholeheartedly in concept that everyone has a right to "life, liberty and the pursuit of happiness." This tends to mean everybody but the company that's after your market share, or the guy who's after the same job you are, or the lady who's trying to get your share of funding for HER project.

A friend of mine is writing a book on conspiracy theories. There are many people and groups of people who spend a great deal of time and energy looking for a responsible party for every negative thing that happens in their lives. My friend's research starts with the Crusades and progresses through World War II and through to the present day with the New World Order. The premise is that every time there are less than optimal conditions (an economic downturn, a drought, a technological change resulting in lost jobs), people point to a demographic or cultural group and say that they are to blame. They proceed to take action-through everything from social and economic discrimination to outright genocide-and feel perfectly justified in doing so. Only afterward does history look back on the situation and recognize the scapegoat scenario that took place.

Hindsight is much easier than clear vision while the situation is in progress.

Most companies have multiple "conspiracy theories" going on at any given time-people seek to explain who is causing the stock price to drop, who's at fault for a project that is taking longer than expected, or why one person was selected for a promotion over another. I've done my share of conjecturing when things haven't gone my way, but every time I have discovered that I either blew it out of proportion or was just plain wrong.

People have always, and will always seek to assign blame for anything negative that happens. Fear is the most prevalent cause of disrespect. According to Andrew Grove, in *Only the Paranoid Survive*, an overwhelming majority of the time, people in business do NOT seek to do harm to another person or company. They're too busy trying to meet their own objectives. Although this is logical, it still surprises us, given the amount of grumbling and gossip every time something goes wrong.

Staying objective about market forces and appreciating the competition's right to exist takes a lot of maturity. More than I've got at some choice moments, I'll admit.

But a basic, respectful, positive approach; along with a genuine desire to "seek first to understand, then to be understood" goes a very long way toward your own success. Being able to separate yourself from the situation and see it from a distance allows you to bring all of your energy, skills and talents to bear on finding the right answers, serving the customer better, and meeting the need at hand. This is a much better use of imaginative power than dreaming up "conspiracy theories."

In this fluid marketplace where people in a given industry tend to change jobs frequently and companies tend to merge or acquire one another, people in conflict tend to "switch sides" more often than not. Tough competitors end up shoulder to shoulder. This can be awkward and downright uncomfortable unless a basic level of respect has been maintained throughout your dealings with one another.

In a dodge ball game in an elementary school gym, kids compete fiercely against the other team, and there is a certain amount of yelling and an occasional accidental bloody nose. But the following week, the teams are mixed up again and former competitors are fast friends against the common "enemy" of the other team (including some of last week's teammates.) Kids typically don't waste a lot of time and energy smoldering over real or imagined slights or fouls. They just want to get down to business and play the game.

The business people I admire the most are in it for this "love of the game" and good sportsmanship. Sportsmanship boils down to the basic respect for your opponent-even to the level of appreciating your opponent for improving your game.

If you can do this all the time, let me know how!

8. On Loving Your Work

In a world that holds books and babies and canyon trails, why should one condemn oneself to live day-in, day-out with people one does not like, and sell oneself to chaperone and correct them?

-Ruth Benedict

In Japan, employees occasionally work themselves to death. It's called Karoshi. I don't want that to happen to anybody in my department. The trick is to take a break as soon as you see a bright light and hear dead relatives beckon.

-Scott Adams

Pleasure in the job puts perfection in the work.

-Aristotle

Okay, so it's not the most loveable thing in the world, some days. There are times when you'd rather be golfing, or touring Europe. There are some days when you'd really rather be having your teeth drilled. But as much as you complain about it, when it comes right down to it, do you love your work?

Work should be a satisfying experience, where you can think hard and implement your thoughts. Work is where you can synthesize, collaborate and create to build things, help people, or create something meaningful.

I love watching Kirk Muspratt, the Canadian symphony orchestra conductor. There is a man who loves his work. You can see it in the respect he shows to the music, to the author of the music, (who is generally dead and long past caring what a 20th century conductor thinks of his work!) to the musicians, and to the audience. He knows that each element in that chain of events is a vital participant in creating something unspeakably beautiful.

Of course, we can't all conduct symphonies. But whatever we do, we can make it an art form. Have you ever noticed a waitress in a restaurant who was truly an artist? One who takes great pride in the experience that each customer has while under her care? That waitress has the opportunity to create many beautiful moments for people—she provides a subtle but important contribution to business meetings over lunch, lovers lingering over dessert, friends resolving a conflict over coffee, and families with busy schedules sharing moment of togetherness over a rare meal together.

There are a lot of things that keep us from enjoying work-a stifling company culture, sustained or artificial stress levels, people on power trips. If these add up to the point where you dread Mondays, it may be time to re-evaluate and seriously consider a different calling or circumstance. Being in a job you hate is a losing proposition-you lose precious time, your self-confidence is eroded, and the company is getting less from its people than they're capable of. If it's not bad enough to throw in the towel, there are some things you can do to improve nearly any job.

If you're a manager, read this for your personal benefit, but also from the perspective of encouraging and enabling your people to love their work. Set an example yourself, and recognize ingenuity and creativity in applying these ideas.

- Improve the aesthetics of your workspace. Some things you may not consciously notice in your day-to-day busy-ness, like dim hallways or dirty carpet have a very real impact on the attitudes of yourself and the people you deal with.

- Get a lamp, or put higher-wattage bulbs in existing fixtures. Good lighting improves your mood, and the mood of people visiting your space. Bring a plant or piece of artwork that lifts your mood.

- Personalize your work. To whatever extent possible, (within the standards and guidelines of your company) find ways to exercise your unique talents and abilities. This can be as subtle as adding a great, inspiring quotation to the end of your e-mail signature line, or as grand as revamping the workflow to add value over the way things have "always been done."

- Get to know your customers and/or coworkers. You can usually find SOMETHING to like about even the most disagreeable specimens. Learn what you can from other people. Mingle with different folks; don't always have your coffee with the same crowd, especially if they're the types that whine a lot. Making each coffee break a complaining contest is an easy habit to get into, but it drains everyone's energy and draws his or her attention to the negatives. And unfortunately, you may acquire a reputation for being one of the "whiners" by association, even if you just sit and listen!

- Address the parts of your job that you don't like. Get disagreeable tasks done first thing in the morning so that you're not dreading them all day. Reward yourself for getting them done. Set up a friendly competition with a co-worker. Or delegate or negotiate to get rid of the things you don't like to do. Find someone who actually enjoys those types of tasks with whom you could trade for something you're good at.

- Keep learning new things. Talk to people, (especially people from different companies and backgrounds to see how they do things differently.) Subscribe to magazines, read books, and surf the Web about issues pertinent to your industry and skill set. There is an amazing amount of information out there that you can apply to do your job better, or learn how it fits into the larger picture of the culture or economy.

- Network and keep abreast of other companies and openings in your field. Even if you're perfectly happy where you are, it's good to know what your alternatives are. This way you go to work every day from the perspective of working where you choose to work, rather than where you feel you have to work.

- Study athletes, musicians, teachers, and businesspeople that love what they do. See how it affects them and makes them better at it by sheer force of attitude. Remember that love is a verb-think and act positively and positive results will follow. Not always immediately, but very reliably and powerfully in ways you may not expect.

9. ON COACHES AND MENTORS

Learning is finding out what we already know. Doing is demonstrating that you know it. Teaching is reminding others that they know just as well as you. You are all learners, doers and teachers.

-Richard Bach

A master can tell you what he expects of you. A teacher, though, awakens your own expectations.

-Patricia Neal

You've got education, skills, energy, and a positive attitude and are hitting the ground in your career very well. Maybe you've got a couple of successes under your belt—deadlines met and projects finished. You're getting to know the ropes of who can help or hinder your projects, and how to get around them.

Are these all of the things that you need?

Although there is no such thing as a self-made person (everyone has people that have contributed to his or her success) there are a lot of people who claim a lot of credit for their own success in business. These are people who think they have clawed their way to the top by sheer skill, wits and awareness.

But anyone who has achieved any level of success will find, upon reflection, that it was the concerted efforts of many teachers, mentors, helpers and employees that helped them along.

A good coach or mentor will save you years of effort by:

- Bringing you and your work to the attention of the right people.

- Pointing out words, phrases and points of style that may work better.

- Telling you about similar projects or efforts that have been tried and succeeded, or tried and failed.

- Helping you polish your presentations-adding a professional, knowledgeable touch that lends credibility.

- Being a safe "sounding board" for thoughts and ideas to help you get the rough edges off them before presenting them to the rest of the world.

How do you find such a godsend? There is an old proverb "when the student is ready, the teacher will appear." However, you may need to help that process along by putting some thought into what type of relationship you want-a coaching relationship or a mentoring relationship. You will probably also want to determine how formal you want that relationship to be. For the sake of discussion, here are some differences.

Coach

- Helps you work through universal issues that would be good in any industry-professional etiquette, management skills, etc.

- Is completely objective – since they work for a different company or department, you don't have to worry about becoming a pawn in their agenda.

- Coaching may be done face-to-face or long distance (by e-mail, for example) on a weekly or monthly basis.

Mentor

- Someone in your field and in your area, that knows the players and the playing field.

- Mentors are generally people who work day-to-day in the industry (probably even the same company) that you are in, and provide more direct feedback.

- You may share a common "agenda" with your mentor (such as promoting a particular concept or project within your company.)

In either case, a coach or mentor must be someone who has attained the level of success that you're shooting for next, and must be someone whose values and principles you share. Look for coaches or mentors in your work-talk with co-workers about senior people they admire. Read trade magazines for articles written by people who strike a chord with you. Read company newsletters for information about people who are recognized for accomplishments.

Also decide on the formality of the relationship. If you want a formal relationship with a coach that will be there at your convenience, you may be better off hiring one. Make sure you go through a reputable firm that can supply references. Mentors generally can't be hired, since they must be someone in your own industry and area. But some progressive companies offer mentoring programs where senior people are formally paired up with midlevel and sometimes entry-level folks withfolks with specific objectives and reporting arrangements.

Do you want to have somebody that you just drop in on (or drop an e-mail to) whenever you have a question? Would you rather set up weekly or monthly meetings over breakfast, lunch, or coffee? Should it be someone in your company that you work with every day, or would you rather have somebody a bit more detached and objective? *Note*: You may want to choose someone who is NOT in your direct reporting line. This way you get broader visibility, and have a safer place to air some issues that you may not want to tell your boss.

The hardest part comes after you have decided on the type of teaching relationship you want and have identified the ideal person for the job. You have to (horrors!) approach that person and find out if they are willing to spend some time with you.

Sometimes these relationships happen naturally. You meet a senior person while working on a project, and then when you both move on to bigger and better things, you keep the relationship open so that you're still collaborating on strategies, and commiserating on problems. Cultivate those relationships-they are worth their weight in gold.

If you do need to start from scratch in approaching a "teacher figure," you may start by introducing yourself, and indicating that you've heard they've had some success or experience with something similar to what you're working on. Ask if they would be interested in looking over a paper or schematic you've done. Keep things simple, and respect their time. If you hit it off, offer to help them with something you're good at (diagrams or Gantt charts, for example) in exchange for some advice about the industry (or whatever you're looking for.)

When you've found a coach or mentor, always respect their time and be sure to show your appreciation for their advice and contributions.

You probably won't take every word of their advice to heart immediately. I've made it a practice to send a note card to one of my old mentors every time something he's said has turned out to be useful.

10. On Networking vs Gossip

If all men knew what others say of them, there would not be four friends in the world.

-Blaise Pascal

Networking is a term used in this context for cultivating relationships with people in your company or industry. These relationships bring mutually beneficial information such as sales leads, job opportunities, and collaboration on solving mutual problems; as well as satisfying friendships and camaraderie.

Gossip, on the other hand, as defined by Webster's, is 1) a person who habitually reveals personal or sensational facts 2) a rumor of an intimate nature.

Granted, some of the information you get (or give) your networking contacts in this age of corporate cannibalism might be sensational. But habitually engaging in gossip, particularly of a negative nature, is damaging to yourself as well as the entities you gossip about. Your contacts may hesitate to share information with you if there is any doubt in their mind of your judgment or integrity-if they have any reason to fear where the information they pass along to you will show up later.

How do you know when you've stepped over the line? Here are some questions you can ask yourself about the information you're sharing.

- Do you have firsthand knowledge that the information is true? Many times information passed along is taken to be true by those receiving it—even if disclaimers surround it.

- How is the person receiving this information likely to use it? Will that use cause undue damage to any person or entity?

- Are you including details just because they are interesting? Are those "interesting details" things that you would mind having shared if you were the subject?

- Will the subject of the information be viewed more positively or negatively?

- Do you find yourself searching for ways to top your contacts for interesting information? One-upmanship – trying to provide more interesting or sensational information tends to cross the line.

- Was the information given to you in confidence? If so, you may have some tough ethical questions of whether that confidence is worth more than the good or harm of sharing the information. Breaching even an informal confidence will certainly ruin your credibility with your source (you have to assume they will know of it) and probably with a number of other people. Breaching a formal confidence could result in legal liability.

We're all human, and we work with other humans. We are interested in each other's jobs and lives and a certain amount of sharing news is part of the enjoyment of our careers. We form alliances with one another, and we like to help one another when we can. We all enjoy talking about each other-learning from and being inspired by stories of what others have done. The questions above are helpful, but the real litmus test is intention.

Scrutinize your motives regularly and you can prevent your own personal network from slipping into a negative pattern that does more harm than good.

11. ON STRUCTURE

When you look at pure structure, a tomato trellis and a birdcage bear some resemblance to one another. They are both made of wire and have horizontal and vertical elements.

Looking at intention and application, however, they are very different. The cage's purpose to confine and restrict movement. The trellis is built to support growth in a particular direction.

The structure of your company probably bears some similarity to both, but the typical corporate structure places too much emphasis on restriction and too little on growth. The ideal structure's primary function is to support growth. Biology tells us that everything is always in a state of growth or decay-so be very selective about what you restrict and why. Pare the restricting elements down to the bare minimum. Determine the rules you have to have to keep you in compliance with regulatory agencies, and to protect your company from a misguided or malicious action of an employee.

Do some brainstorming on the potential pitfalls, legal and practical; and put supports in place to protect the company from damage. Consult with an attorney and an accountant. Put the checks and balances into place to "encourage honesty" on everyone's part. Once the checks and balances are in place, focus your attention on growth, rather than restriction. Ensure that employees have the support they need to make decisions, serve customers, and produce products with a minimum of bureaucracy. Give them as much control over their piece of the business as you possibly can.

We've found that people are much more motivated, inventive and effective when they are given more ownership and latitude than they are accustomed to. Make sure that everyone understands the big picture of where they fit in the company, participates in quality control, and to whatever extent possible under the circumstances-shares in the profits when they contribute to the bottom line.

Participate in the growth of your employees as they participate in the growth of the company. Provide training opportunities on topics that are vital and relevant to your company. Set up a formal or informal network of coaching and mentoring. Promote from within. Provide non-monetary incentives such as flexible hours, the option of working from home, or better facilities based on individual, team or company performance. (Company performance can be based on quarterly earnings, volume of products shipped, or some other measurement of success) Keep pace with the growth of your company in all areas. Don't allow a bottleneck in supplies or equipment to cause stagnation in any part of your company.

You can't blow out all the stops and grow uncontrolled, but manage and direct the growth rather than allowing it to be blocked. Although a cage and a trellis are built of the same materials and have some of the same structural elements, they serve very different purposes. Corporate structures can be built for large companies or small, can be team based or hierarchical, can be steeply vertical or flat as Kansas. Any structure can be (and probably has been, under the right circumstances) wildly successful. The shape and materials don't matter as much as the intention and application. Give your company the protection and support it needs but still has room to grow.

12. ON SILOS

This is happiness: To be dissolved into something completely great.
-Willa Cather

Overachievers tend to work alone. Having to do a "group project" often makes them frantic. They are extremely uncomfortable until they have the opportunity to carve off a piece of the project they can call their own. They go off into their own corner and complete the work by themselves, and then bring it back to merge with the other pieces at the last possible moment.

The image of working in a narrowly defined space where you act independently and can't see what others are doing brings to mind a group of grain silos-they may be standing together, but their contents don't mix.

Most corporate cultures reward individual achievement. It does relative comparisons of people and skills for raises and layoffs. It grades on a curve. Depending on the group and the timeframe, being able to segment a project can be a very useful survival skill. However, it should not preclude being able to work well in groups.

Working in groups, or at least aligning with other groups and projects allows you to

- Avoid mistakes others have already made
- Leverage effort that has already been expended
- Eliminate gaps between efforts, and ensure that your products are useable by a group in the next "silo"
- Draw from a broader base of skills and experience

- Gain support and "buy-in" for your own projects

- Identify potential problems before customers see them

You can leverage the advantages of collaborative work and still be an excellent individual achiever. Here are some ways to avoid the "silo effect":

- Determine which projects (or parts of your project) are in your best interest to keep to yourself. Usually people are much more secretive than they need to be. Unless there is a reason NOT to share information, share it!

- Set aside at least one day a week to go to lunch with a coworker (preferably a different one each week) with a different perspective from your own. (Note-We've found Fridays to be particularly conducive for this sort of thing because Fridays tend to be more relaxed anyway.)

- Ask for input on a document or plan.

- Hang a flowchart or process map on your cube wall with the heading "Graffiti Welcome"–

- Always be willing to take a few minutes to discuss an issue or problem with a co-worker who requests help. You'd be surprised what you can learn that can help your own issues and problems!

- Be an official or unofficial coach or mentor. Keep your eyes open for good opportunities for others and make introductions or forward openings.

- Socialize at work when the opportunity presents itself! While waiting for meetings to start or waiting for the copy machine, chat about kids and hobbies. As long as it's not out of hand, the time taken from work tends to repay itself in contacts, better relationships, and information.

Focus on your individual performance, but don't isolate yourself! Stay out of the silos.

13. ON "OTHER PEOPLE'S SHOES"

Don't be condescending to unskilled labor. Try it for a half a day first.

-Brooks Atkinson

These days, employers are struggling to find (and keep) quality employees. Employees are struggling to find (and keep) better positions and to have their thoughts and ideas included in the corporate strategy and culture. In these efforts, there has been a lot of posturing, positioning, scheming, conniving, and schmoozing going on, but surprisingly little actual communication.

Communication, by its definition, implies understanding by both parties. The best way to do that is to spend less time on your position (which you probably know very well) and more time understanding the other guy's.

A very powerful event took place in a corporation as the result of a computer mainframe failure. After an emergency session during which the objectives were outlined and a team deployed to perform an emergency replacement, the technical people were very, very busy and management were feeling rather, well, helpless.

The CEO went up to one of the technicians who seemed to have a second between tasks and asked him what he could do to help. After being waved off twice with polite mumblings; the technician realized he was going to have to give this guy something to DO in order to be left alone.

He quickly gave him a bundle of cables and a handful of cable-tags, and a quick explanation of how he wanted the cables tagged. The CEO spent the afternoon, in full view of the frantic staff, tagging cable. He did it wrong at first, and I don't envy the technician who had to explain to the big cheese that he couldn't even tag cable correctly!

In any event, with everyone working together in choreography as complicated as *Swan Lake*, the mainframe was replaced and brought online in record time. The mainframe vendor was even astonished.

This had a big impact on the corporate culture for a long time afterward, and there was much speculation about it, references to it, and analysis around the water cooler for years. But everyone agreed that the act of this CEO was remarkable. He did a number of things (probably not intending all of them at the time.)

- He validated the importance of even the most mundane task.
- He showed respect for his staff by "subordinating" himself to their commands when he was in a technical realm. He acknowledged their position as experts of the situation at hand.
- He demonstrated that even very smart people make mistakes when they're outside their area of expertise, and must rely on their teammates to correct them.

There are other instances where this "role reversal" takes place in corporate culture. Boxing Day in Canada is a holiday created for this reason. Staff members reverse roles on the day after Christmas.

One government office I know has customer service reps "from the trenches" participate in the strategic management meetings. This has a number of advantages on both sides-management gets real information on how things are working and how customers are responding. They also get better communication, understanding and buy-in from the staff.

The customer service reps (who rotate through this position on a three-month basis) get some exposure to strategic management concepts. They begin to understand the challenges of working with budgets, arranging resources to meet seasonal highs and lows, and implementing new or fixing old systems.

Walking in someone else's shoes is not just a cliché. Need more evidence? Many sites on the Internet look like they were built for the amusement of the technical staff, not to serve the needs of customers.

If someone doesn't seem to be getting the point, rather than spending more time finessing your position, you should spend that energy walking a mile in his or her shoes.

14. ON DOORMATS

I am an expert in hookers. I'm an expert in doormats. I'm an expert in victims. They were the best parts. And when I woke up—sociologically, politically, and creatively—I could no longer take those parts and look in the mirror.

-Shirley MacLaine

There is a term called "Malicious Compliance" that refers to doing what you're told to do, even if you know it isn't going to work. This always reminds me of the cartoons where one character is snatched by another and yells "Put me down!" His abductor immediately complies, dropping him out of an airplane or off a cliff.

Being "maliciously compliant" is not without Dilbertesque entertainment value, especially if you don't like your boss and are looking forward to the literal or implied "I told you this wasn't going to work" when the project doesn't yield the results he is expecting. And if your boss is so into doing it "his way" that he won't listen to alternatives, you may not have a choice other than to comply with his requests with malicious (or at least uncommitted) intent.

If you're on the other end of the equation, you may find that your staff does exactly what you tell them to do, and don't employ their expertise and knowledge as much as you would like.

Reasons for Malicious Compliance

Reasons for this vary. People don't want to be seen as complainers or wet blankets. There could be something about your style that implies a command, rather than a request. Your people may come from a traditional command and control culture (there are still a lot of them around) where it is not expected for them to speak up when they know something's not right. In many environments, coming forward with a problem results in personal responsibility for finding a solution, which this person may not have.

Beige People Syndrome

Someone once said that the greatest threat to a corporate culture, or to anyone's individual career, is the "beige people syndrome." Beige people are those that look busy and professional, sound good when they speak at meetings, and accomplish precisely nothing. They don't stand out in any way. They have no original thoughts; no opinions worth standing up for, and make no contributions of any kind. They are a threat because they are expensive, they take up space, they camouflage a profound lack of progress, and, the most insidious characteristic of all-beige ness is contagious.

The real threat is when people in your company see that the "beige people" survive and prosper; while people who have opinions, take risks, and accomplish things are more likely to make mistakes, and therefore risk being disciplined, fired or blackballed. The "safest course," if you want to keep your job, is to take no risks, do what is asked but no more, to display no creativity, and to effect no change.

This is dangerous for a business in today's market. Your competition is doing new and innovative things with technology. They are breaking molds and traditions. They are listening to what customers want, and customers want more, better, faster and cheaper than they did even five years ago.

You need the fully engaged minds, hearts, creativity and energy of your people in order to keep and expand your market share.

Fighting the Invisible Illness

How can you fight malicious compliance and insidious beigeness? Part of the reason they're so insidious is because they are so hard to see. Here are some suggestions.

- Publicly reward innovation. Some companies have programs in place to pay cash for good ideas. United Illuminating, Inc. offers employees 10% of the profits (or savings) from any submitted idea that is implemented. If this isn't possible, provide recognition and kudos for good ideas in whatever forum is appropriate for your organization.

- Keep an "idea notebook." Even if you can't use it right away, record the idea and the contributor and mull them over once in a while. Conditions may change, schedules may free up, and an idea that was impractical three months ago may find its niche today.

- Never "shoot the messenger." The first time a person who brings you news of a problem or potential problem gets impacted in a negative way, word will get around. The result will be that your staff will be more inclined to do what they're told than to raise the red flag when they see an iceberg ahead. (Impacted negatively includes being yelled at, fired, overlooked for promotion, branded a "complainer" or anything of the sort.)

- Structure employee performance reviews on objective criteria-not just "gets along well with others." Require that each employee account for SPECIFIC contributions made during the reporting period. Make sure that raises, promotions, bonuses, etc. take this information into account. Do some digging to make sure people aren't taking credit for other people's work.

- Sometimes the people who are best at making evaluation reports look good are not the biggest contributors. Use objective criteria and apply it to everyone (up and down the management "food chain.")

- Engage the entire staff affected by a project in the planning process. Have a big meeting, hang the project plan on the wall, or post discussion groups on the Intranet to solicit input. There is a story about a computer hardware installation where the programmers, systems people, building management, etc. were all in agreement about what should occur. A janitor, however, noticed that the installation would involve the removal of some tiles that he knew contained asbestos. By "raising the red flag," the janitor caused some vital replanning to avoid those tiles and thus avoid environmental, and potentially legal implications. You never know where a good idea is going to come from. Respect all sources.

- Address these issues directly. Address "malicious compliance" and the "beige people syndrome" in a meeting or on a bulletin board. (The degree of laughter or knowing nods and raised eyebrows may give you a hint that this strikes a chord with your staff.)

- Let people know that the expectation is that people will make individual, creative, enthusiastic contributions to help the company succeed. New ideas are appreciated and rewarded. Blind obedience is not something of value.

- Start the ball rolling by asking the staff for ideas on how to prevent these insidious illnesses.

15. On Skill

A winner is someone who recognizes his God-given talents, works his tail off to develop them into skills, and uses these skills to accomplish his goals.

-Larry Bird

I hate this shallow Americanism which hopes to get rich by credit, to get knowledge by raps on midnight tables, to learn the economy of the mind by phrenology, or skill without study, or mastery without apprenticeship.

-Ralph Waldo Emerson

If you've ever read *Atlas Shrugged*, or anything else by Ayn Rand, for that matter, you've read a very good description of how people with skills or talents are not always rewarded for those abilities. In fact, they're quite often penalized. Not just in the 1940s, when these novels are set, but in today's corporate culture as well.

There are still people who are afraid to hire someone with more skill than they have. The head of a PR department may be hesitant to hire someone who is a better writer than himself, for example, for fear that the new employee will make him obsolete, or at least make him look bad by comparison.

Programmers have been known to make systems more complex than they need to be so that no one can understand them but themselves. This is a perverse form of job security-by designing something so badly that no one else can operate it, they ensure their future.

Organizations suffer from this cowardice. Here are some of the effects.

- Failure to attract and obtain skilled employees
- Existing employees may hide their skills for fear that they will become victims of their boss' paranoia
- Provincialism of information sharing may cause duplicate systems (everybody has their own secret spreadsheet of contact information, instead of an effective, cross-department pool)
- Localization of policies and procedures that are much more complex than they need to be.
- Inability to function if a certain employee goes on vacation or leaves the company.

Good leaders understand that by building a powerful staff, and by giving credit where credit is due for a job well done or for an insightful idea, they also make themselves look good. There is not a set number of kudos to go around that people in a company need to compete for.

Positive actions breed positive actions. Skilled departments that are good at what they do can always find more and different ways they can help the company, and thus expand their influence.

A very wise manager told me that the ultimate goal in any job is to make yourself obsolete. Find a way to automate the job; find a way to teach less experienced or skilled (less expensive) people to do it; find someone to whom you can outsource it for less than what you're making. The caveat was that as long as we continued to do this, the manager would continually find us new and exciting things to do, and keep us progressing up our chosen career path.

This obviously took a great deal of trust. It would be easy to "downsize" an employee that had found a more efficient way to replace himself. But, in this case he kept his word.

Even in organizations where this wasn't "the deal," I've found it to be a good practice to work myself out of a job. Find a way to document it, automate it, and make it easier, find a person whom I can teach that wants to move "up the ladder," and then inform my boss that I need something new to do to amuse myself. Luckily, I've always had good bosses.

Value the skills in your company. Cultivate a learning environment. Reward those that learn and teach others. Reward cooperative efforts, consolidation of information and process building. This might take some imagination on your part, especially if you're in a lean phase. Find new, exciting projects for people who automate their jobs, teach others to do them, or otherwise "make themselves obsolete." That way, everybody wins.

16. ON BALANCE

Be aware of wonder. Live a balanced life—learn some and think some and draw and paint and sing and dance and play and work every day some.

-Robert Fulghum

The dinosaur's eloquent lesson is that if some bigness is good, an overabundance of bigness is not necessarily better.

-Eric A. Johnston

Everyone I know is struggling with the balance between his or her work and home life. I am too. There is always the temptation to take a document home to look it over one more time before it's presented to an important client. There is also the temptation to play hooky and go with your kid's class to the zoo. We have a limited amount of time and a lot to accomplish on a lot of different fronts.

Most of us live with our feet in different worlds, as it were. We're fulfilling different roles. And yet to be successful in any of these areas we need undivided focus.

The simplest way to do this is to set your hours-you work 8 to 5; the rest of your time belongs to you and your family. You focus your undivided attention on your work during work hours and yourself and your hobbies or family "after hours."

Well, that worked fine ten years ago, but now the expectation is to travel more, work longer hours, and to continue your education.

Meanwhile, the demands of having relationships, families, children and communities are not diminishing.

Rising youth violence, drugs and gangs tell us that we need to spend more time with our kids. Rising divorce rates tell us we need to spend more time in our relationships. We still have parents, grandparents, brothers, sisters, aunts, uncles, neighbors and friends—and the holidays are coming up!

The Asian concept of balance is shown in the yin-yang symbol. (This is a circle with two sections, black and white.) The two sections are equal, but the circle is not clearly divided in half. There is a curve bisecting the circle. In addition, two smaller sections of color are incorporated into the larger sections. The concept is very fluid.

A depiction of the same concept from a Western philosophy would probably be to cut the circle neatly in half by bisecting it with a straight line. That would be cleaner and simpler. Life is not always clean and simple, and almost never involves straight lines.

I think we complicate life more by expecting it to be clean and simple.

The circle just doesn't bisect neatly. There is no straight line between our roles. We don't have multiple personalities.

The key is to focus on the center. Which are your core beliefs and principles? What is important to you? What are your characteristics? Do the parts of your life align with those values and characteristics?

Your roles may be very different from one another. You may have to go, in a single afternoon, from prosecuting capital murder cases to hosting a tea party for 4-year-old girls. But if both of those roles align with your basic values-both of them are centered on using your skills to make the world a better place according to your values, then it doesn't take as much energy as doing something you hate or that you disagree with, even if it's something expected of you.

In many non-Western philosophies things do not have to divide exactly 50:50 in order to balance. 30:70, or even 10:90 is acceptable. The apparent imbalance is resolved by a third factor-time. Over time, things divide themselves differently and the 30:70 becomes 70:30. Or 90:10. Whatever is required of the situation has a way of naturally resolving itself if you focus on the center rather than on the boundaries between sections.

Over the holidays, you may find yourself spending more time with your family and not being so driven at work. That's okay. You probably have it coming from all the times you got home late or brought work home.

There has been an artificial division between work and home that started with the Industrial Revolution. Prior to that time, everyone's home life and work life was pretty much the same thing. In a rural economy, the success of the farm was the family's prosperity. Everyone worked together and there was no division.

The pendulum is swinging back toward that type of unity. More people choosing flextime, work at home, or exercise telecommuting options. Companies have "Bring Your Daughter To Work Day" and sponsoring school events and activities.

Being less rigid in our divisions and our thinking gives us more options to be successful in all of our roles. Here are some ideas:

- Have "homework time" a couple times a week, when everyone (maybe in the living room or around the kitchen table) works on their own homework—kids work on school work, reading, or completing their own projects. Adults work on "homework" from work, research, or study for classes they are taking. This provides for some togetherness-you're there for each others' questions and problems, you demonstrate that good work habits are important for grownups as well as kids, and you get stuff done!

- Discuss your day around dinner. Not just "How was your day?" "Oh, fine." But involve your family in the challenges, opportunities, puzzles and successes of your work. They will open up and be more inclined to share their challenges, opportunities, puzzles and successes at their work or school. (Be sure to listen more than you talk, especially with younger children.) You learn more about each other and might get some interesting insights that you may be too close to the situation to see. Some really great insights come from spouses or children who are seeing the situation from a different frame of reference.

- Don't waste your energy feeling guilty. Make your decision about what is most important at the moment based on the circumstances and then BE THERE. Whether you're in an emergency after-hours meeting at work; or in the stands at your kid's softball game; or at lunch with your spouse: any time you spend thinking about other things you should be doing is completely wasted-it doesn't do anyone any good. Devote your attention completely to the people and situation at hand. Even if you decided wrong, cut your losses by making good use of the time you've committed. Chances are, by fully investing your efforts now you can "buy" some time later for your other roles.

Although there will always be a limited amount of time and a lot to accomplish, there are also a lot of ways to make the balance between career and family a good one. One of the best is to spend less time and energy agonizing over it, drawing boundaries where none exist (or need to exist) and spending that energy instead on being fully committed to enjoy the various roles we've made for ourselves.

17. On Cookie Cutter Techniques

The secret of happiness is to find a congenial monotony.

-V. S. Pritchett

Working with someone who falls victim to the latest fad in management is an interesting experience.

Working with someone who hasn't changed methods in 20 years is equally interesting.

Whether this person reports to you or you report to him or her (and to a lesser extent if you're peers) you've probably been frustrated by the vacillations of the "flavor of the month" style of management. Or you've been frustrated by the inflexibility that doesn't take into account that 20 years of advancements have been made in management science.

There is an old proverb-"Beware the man who has read one book." (The emphasis being on the "one.") Someone completely dependent on a single philosophy of management, or sold on a program, gimmick, or tool, can be dangerous to his company. Even if the technique or tool is basically sound, it becomes a crutch that prevents dealing with issues creatively, being open to input from people, and adapting to the situation at hand. Whether the manager is "sold" on that methodology or program for a week, a month, or 20 years, that dependence is a symptom and a cause of weakness in a management professional.

There are good programs out there-There's the 7-Habit Series by Stephen Covey, the One Minute Manager series by Spencer Johnson et. al., the Tao of (Leadership, Management, etc.), there's the Deming

54

Quality Assurance Approach, the Knowledge Management approach, and of course the Idiots or Dummies approaches to management.

There are tools galore-Gantt Charts, Pert Charts, Franklin Planner inserts, software that delineates critical path, software that tracks individual time and performance, software that tracks costs, (some that do more than one of these functions) and thousands of other books, programs, tools, and seminars. Many of those mentioned have a great deal of merit and are worth looking into.

No tool or technique of them should completely dominate your way of doing business. (Not even this book!)

How can you leverage new techniques and tools effectively without going overboard?

- Outline your goals and objectives independently. Your business is unique. It serves a specialized market niche or it wouldn't exist. Determine what unique opportunities and risks your business entails, then your goals and objectives become your overriding concerns. If you choose to use tools and methods to reach those goals and objectives, select the ones that are the most consistent and relevant to YOUR business or industry.

- Be open to new tools and methods on the market, but shop carefully. Get your information from more than one INDEPENDENT source. (Books, seminars, Internet sites, trade magazines, etc.) Investigate before you buy. Talk to clients that have implemented the solution you're considering. Discuss the similarities and differences with your situation.

- Evaluate automated tools from different vendors. The trend in the industry is toward standardization, so you may be able to "mix and match" to get the best set of tools to meet the unique needs of your business. (Be careful, though, because too much customization in software can make your system more difficult and expensive to maintain. When in doubt, get competent technical advice from an independent source.)

- Communicate with your people. Get their input and allow them to participate in the implementation of any new product or system. Make sure they have the opportunity for input BEFORE you commit to a particular system. You may want to form a cross-functional team to "shop" for tools that meet a particular objective. The people "in the trenches" will be the first to see the red flags, or potential opportunities for added benefit that you might not see from your angle.

- On the same note, be honest about techniques you've read about. Distribute books, literature, newsletters, etc. and promote discussion of their merits. People are much more receptive of management philosophies that are adopted by the company if they understand them, as opposed to feeling like management is "using some technique ON them" to make them comply.

- Have a backup waiting for every system you use (for time tracking, task tracking, finance tracking, etc.) Put the time in before you're in a crisis to decide what to do if, for whatever reason, your system fails. Even if your plan is to "wing it," decide on the points of departure (and plans to get back into your chosen system) before a situation arises.

No matter how good the books, methodologies, seminars, software and programs are, there is no substitute for good old-fashioned creativity, resourcefulness and rational thought in a manager. Independent thought is risky and difficult, since you're putting your own thoughts out there for people to criticize. But independent thought is the only component of management skill that cannot be replicated by a program or a computer system. You can (and should!) automate the way(s) you get and organize information, but the evaluation and decision-making you do with that information requires real human ingenuity.

Think hard, strategically and independently, for at least an hour out of every business day. (This isn't the first time we've recommended this, but for other reasons.) Keep a notebook of risks, opportunities, and ideas; whether you use them now or later, or not at all. Talk to people in your industry, or in your own business, who see things from different angles.

Get your information from as many sources as possible, but don't pay too much attention to where it comes from. Some of the best ideas come from a billboard, from your kids, or from a stray conversation on an unrelated topic.

Ironically, the more books you read, classes or seminars you go to, or software you evaluate, the more independent your thinking will become. You are synthesizing information and using it for your own purposes, rather than simply conforming to a "cookie cutter" technique designed by and for someone else.

18. On Important Distractions

You can always find a distraction if you're looking for one.
-Tom Kite

You can't be world-class at everything. Now more than ever before, you need to focus on the core competency that makes your business uniquely better than every other. You need to direct as much time, attention and energy on that "focus point" or core competency as possible. Picture a hundred people pushing on a brick wall with their hands. Now picture the force of a hundred people being focused behind a tool, like a sledgehammer, at that same brick wall. Focus is power. Diffusion is weakness.

So what do you do with all of the distracting details? Every business has a lot of "support functions" that may not contribute directly to the bottom line, but they need to be done in order to keep the doors open, keep the employees paid, keep taxes and invoices paid, etc. etc. etc.

It may be time to take a hard look at business functions and determine what is really contributing to the bottom line and which functions could be streamlined, handled differently, outsourced or redeployed in a different structure.

Many smaller, newer companies and startups have the advantage of bringing new and different products and services to market better, faster and cheaper because they are not saddled with decades of years of superfluous stuff.

They don't have a receptionist; they have an answering service (automated or outsourced) that screens calls.

They don't have an army of administrative people to do typing and filing; they've instead had all of their sales reps learn a system of documentation using computer files.

They don't have a big accounting department. They keep their own simple books using a software program, and they have a professional service look over and file their quarterly taxes.

There are companies (some very successful because of their concentrated focus) that specialize on a particular support function. They focus on learning everything there is to know about fulfillment and shipping, for example. And because it's all they do, they can take advantage of economies of scale and do it better, cheaper and faster than a three person-department in an older company with antiquated equipment and less-than adequate training.

If it's a "Core Competency" for your company, you need to devote the resources to make it world-class. If it's not a core competency, find a way get out of it.

On the other extreme, you don't want to divest your company of all support functions pell-mell and lay off a bunch of people, either. That won't make you popular with the community you live in, the press, your vendors, or your clients. We've all heard horror stories about a company that outsourced their payroll or shipping and ended up spending everything they saved and then some fixing errors and rebuilding relationships with offended employees or clients.

It may be time to take a hard look at support functions, but it's also time to take a hard look at how to reorganize them to meet your needs today. Here are some ideas:

- Think win-win, especially for support employees. You may be able to redesign or even eliminate a small, non-productive department by redeploying those personnel into other areas of the company. Offer training, promotions and other incentives to those that want newer, more marketable skills. In return, you get experienced, dependable employees with broader knowledge of your company's workings. (It's often easier to teach a good employee a skill than to teach a skilled person to be a good employee!)

- If you outsource a department, you may be able to "outsource" the employees, too. Many specialty firms would welcome your old employees along with the contract to provide you service, since they have client-specific knowledge. In return, your support personnel get to work for a larger company in their own field who can offer them better opportunities for training and advancement.

If you decide to work with a service provider to do your payroll, accounting, shipping, or other support function, shop very, very carefully.

- Make sure that the lines of communication are wide open. Be sure that they're comfortable with you talking to the people actually doing the work, not a 'single point of entry' like a sales rep.

- Find out what their problem resolution process is, and how quickly they turn around a problem or request. Are they available evenings and weekends when a customer or employee has a problem?

- Write the contract so that they have some financial incentive to perform well. Using a Service Level Agreement with financial incentives and disincentives (they get paid bonuses if they meet or exceed expectations, and are docked if they mess up) is a very good way to ensure that they stay motivated to help you succeed. Service Level Agreements take some creativity and planning to write and to enforce, but they generally are a good deal for both parties.

- Cultivate relationships that "blur the lines" between your company and the companies that provide you with products and services. Dell (the computer maker) has such good relationships with its suppliers that it keeps its inventory of parts down to a minimum, using JIT (Just in Time). This helps their cash flow, and also helps both Dell and its suppliers take advantage of technological advances by getting new components into their products and out to consumers faster and cheaper.

Many older companies fail to take advantage of opportunities because they are afraid of changing, reorganizing, and outsourcing. IBM simply would not consider laying off an employee for many years, until they found themselves at risk of losing more than they had ever bargained for.

Don't be afraid to reduce or eliminate the distractions, so that you can focus the lion's share of your people's time and energy on your bottom line, as you remember that those "distractions" are still vitally important, so the redeploying, outsourcing or streamlining must be done very intelligently.

19. ON SAFETY NETS

Mishaps are like knives that either serve us or cut us as we grasp them by the blade or the handle.

-James Russell Lowell

In these changing, uncertain times, it's easy to play the ostrich maneuver, bury yourself in day-to-day work, and hope that the changes don't target YOU.

Corporate acquisitions, takeovers, business failures, mergers, and so forth tend not to discriminate. It's possible to do everything right, and still have the ground slide out from under you. This is not a reassuring thought.

If you realize what your real security is, and take steps to build it while times are good, you will have more options when changes bring their sometimes unsettling (sometimes downright frightening!) mix of challenges and opportunities.

Your real security lies in your professional expertise, your network of contacts, and your personal level of preparedness. Cultivate all of these things, in good times and bad. You will probably find that having the added security gives you the guts to take the well-considered risks and be more successful, even when things are going well.

Professional Expertise

Your professional expertise should be current, documented, and varied.

* Study trends in your field and find out how advances in science and technology are changing your field, and find out how you can see

where the demand will be in two, five, and ten years. Stay ahead of the curve.

- Note-most people have at least two fields these days. An accounting specialist working for a manufacturing company should stay abreast of developments in both accounting and manufacturing. A call center or fulfillment rep in a retail industry should read up on both call centers and retail.

- Make sure your professional expertise is documented-if you know a lot about a particular topic, pursue a degree, certification, or at least some formal experience with that topic so that it merits real mention on your resume. Update your resume at least once every six months so that it's always presentable at a moment's notice. Many people keep their resume' in several databases or on the Web constantly, even when they're happy with their job. You never know when something better will come along, or when something good will disappear.

- Note: 20 years ago this type of "advertising" might have been interpreted as disloyalty or unhappiness with a job. Nowadays, most enlightened managers assume their people are always looking, and would rather have employees that are with their company by choice-that choice being made on a weekly, monthly or yearly basis.

- Most really successful people are constantly learning something new-whether it's related to their field or not. In fact, some of the executives to employ are those that have wide-ranging interests-from being avid tennis players to painting ceramic vases. This "liberal education," even (and especially) if it's self-directed, provides an outlet for stress, will allow you to bring a rich set of perspectives to the table when planning or solving problems.

- Cultivate a hobby or interest (something you enjoy) into a way to make money. You may never need or want to make a full-time occupation of it, but you can learn a lot that can help you in your "day job" by starting a small business, even as an academic exercise. You may want to involve your kids and teach them (or let them research and then teach you!) about business and economics.

Contacts

Your network of contacts is one of the most valuable assets you have, in your current job as well as providing a wide network of possibilities if you need to make a change.

- Don't just dust off your Rolodex when you think you're getting canned. Take the time to cultivate relationships, share ideas, and support one another—find excuses to stay in contact. Remember birthdays and anniversaries, send congratulations for successes you hear about through the grapevine or read in trade publications. Forward a particularly interesting clipping or Internet address for something you find that you know would be interesting to their line of work or hobby.

- Never refuse a favor if you can help it. Make every effort to help a person who asks for assistance. You never know when you'll need a favor in return, and word gets around among people whether you believe in Karma or not.

- Cultivate a varied network of contacts-not just in your field, but also in related fields, or fields you have an interest in. Especially if you have a 'niche job' with a fairly narrow market, you may be more secure if you can expand your contacts and experiences.

- Join professional organizations, community organizations, and other groups. Being well known in your professional and geographical community won't hurt.

Personal Preparedness

Ensuring that your family's needs are met is every person's number one priority. Many people have felt "trapped" in a bad job or ethical situation they didn't like because of a lack of options in this area. The better you prepare, the better able you are to exercise options without impacting yours or your family's financial situation.

- Keep a financial safety cushion. This should go without saying.

- Live below your means, within reason. Pretend you have to live on a percentage of your current income. The remainder can be used to accumulate your safety cushion, provide for additional education (or the time to obtain it) or help you sustain an unexpected loss of any kind. If you're roped into an expensive house, car, and other financial obligations, you become chained rather inflexibly to a high income or cash flow.

- Study your options for benefits. Retirement, insurance, and other financial benefits are all replaceable, at a price. Find out what the markets are and how much you would need to make if one or more of your company-provided benefits were to become unavailable for whatever reason. Many people who work for companies or government agencies become "addicted" to the benefits and find it difficult to leave, even when circumstances dictate that they should.

- Take care of yourself and your family, from a physical, emotional and spiritual standpoint. If you're all frazzled, time-deprived, sleep-deprived and snapping at one another; you'll probably only make things worse for one another during any kind of career wrinkle despite your best intentions. Walking on eggshells can be very draining, and can make a tense situation really unbearable. But if you have a history of being supportive of one another in little, everyday ways as well as big, life-changing ones; you have an unmatchable source of strength.

These are all very obvious net-weaving strategies. Sometimes the obvious things are the ones that we overlook. Go through this list now and identify and mend any holes you see, while you're thinking about it.

20. On Finding Your Desk

One of the advantages of being disorderly is that one is constantly making exciting discoveries.

-A. A. Milne

We live in a paperless society. Yeah, right! Look at my desk!

The computer I'm sitting at right now is capable of storing 3 gigabytes (Actually, 3,249,307,648 bytes) of data. It contains applications that let me sort, find, store, alter, print, send and manipulate that data in lots of ways that I could never imagine a use for.

So why is my desk still covered with paper? I have manuscripts to review, letters to answer, photographs to scan, bills to pay, a printout of a web page from a piece of software I want to download, magazines with little blue tags sticking out of them indicating that there's something in there I'm supposed to read, project binders to update; and a cup of coffee.

All this administrivia can be paralyzing. It's hard to come up with the next innovative, creative new project or solution to a problem when you're drowning in details. There have been times when I felt like I could use three personal assistants. At others, I would be incapable of delegation because I didn't know where to start.

Here are some ideas that have worked for me (although I obviously still have a ways to go!)

Divide and Conquer

Most talented people enjoy what they do, at least more than they enjoy paperwork. When you're really on a roll with a project, closing a big deal, working out a problem, or designing a fabulous new system; the last thing you want to be bothered with is writing that status report or filing that expense claim.

Four and one-half days a week, I do my "job." I meet with clients and co-workers, work on projects, write articles, read and review relevant industry publications, etc. Any administrative paperwork task that comes my way that is not directly related to my job gets dumped into a box.

One-half day a week (Friday mornings, generally) I block out my schedule to go through the box and take care of each item in it. I attempt to handle each item to completion (to a permanent file, or the "round file") before setting it down. This way I don't have a backlog of miscellaneous things. I also take care of other things that I consider "paperwork," even if they aren't on paper. Filing time and expenses on my company's automated system, writing and filing a status report online, update my files, archiving e-mail, and so forth. (These end up on paper, as line items in my day planner, anyway.)

You may want to divide this up to one hour a day, or one day a month, or whatever suits your needs. I've found that I don't dread the paperwork as much if it isn't an intrusion on my "real job." It's worth sacrificing half a day if it gives me four-and-a-half days of uninterrupted, creative bliss.

Hide

When you have a lot of administrative or paperwork tasks to do, find a place you won't be interrupted with something more tempting. At a minimum, shut your office door (if you have one.) Set your phone to voicemail. Find an unused conference room. Work at home. Jeffrey J. Fox (*CEO*) recommends going to the library one day a month to do undisturbed "homework."

The caveat to working somewhere other than your office (if you can manage to do that) is that you have to make sure you have everything you need. Bring your laptop computer, calculator, extra batteries, envelopes, stamps, phone directory, day planner, coffee, peppermints, and everything else you imagine you could need to be productive. Finding yourself without the appropriate tools just gives you another excuse to let the pile grow.

Schedule It

Many people assume that if they whittle away at their administrative tasks in their "spare time" between appointments, that it will get done. If that works for you, great, I find that I end up using most of my "spare time," if there is any-talking to people, handling phone calls and other immediate things that come up. Putting the finishing touches on a presentation for the next meeting, etc. etc. etc. I would never get around to the paperwork if it weren't a "regularly scheduled" agenda item.

If I put off the paperwork for more than a week (this varies depending on the paperwork required in your world) I begin to dread it. The pile becomes huge, some items are late anyway and won't receive a glowing reception, and I've set a precedent. If I've put it off this long, one more day won't matter.

Automate It

The inertia of a stagnant pile of paper takes more energy to overcome than a small, regularly turned over mound.

Evaluate how you spend your administrative time. Is there anything you do repetitively? Do you have more than one system that handles the same thing? Do you have to copy things more than once?

You may find it worth your while to examine and automate the process. If you find yourself typing or writing the same thing more than once a day, write a macro to type it for you. Get labels or a stamp made.

Isolate your administrative, "paperwork" tasks. Find a place to do them, and schedule the time to crank them out regularly. By doing this you can free up most (or at least more) of your time to be more creative, effective, people-oriented, responsive, professional, and everything else you want to be.

21. On "Business Parties"-

Meetings...are rather like cocktail parties. You don't want to go, but you're cross not to be asked.

-Jilly Cooper

Chances are, you'll probably end up with invitations to a few holiday get-togethers that are work-related. How you handle them can be a great advantage or disadvantage. One thing that every businessperson learns very young is that some of these parties bear very little resemblance to the Dickens-like family or social gatherings that characterize the season. Only companies that are very small or very enlightened can enjoy these types of parties where everyone is there for the sole purpose of enjoying one anothers company.

Opinions on the topic vary, between those who recommend avoiding parties and those who feel that they are an ideal opportunity.

In his book *How to Become CEO*, Jeffrey J. Fox suggests skipping all office parties, and giving polite excuses. Or, if you must attend for fear of offending someone, put in a forty-five minute appearance (with your spouse, if spouses are invited) drink a soft drink, thank the person who invited you, and leave with polite excuses. He indicates that spending your social time relaxing and having fun with friends and family is a much safer and more productive way to spend your time during the holidays.

His reasoning is that holiday parties can be the cause of a lot of problems. People get carried away with alcohol or "letting their hair down" in other ways and say and do things they shouldn't. Those same people resent other partygoers simply for being witnesses to their bad behavior. Spouses may become uncomfortable or downright offended by being included in (or excluded from) well-meaning jokes. Even if you personally behave yourself, you may be blamed for (or be a witness to) the foibles of others.

D. A. Benton, in **Lions Don't Need to Roar**, takes a different opinion-gatherings of any type are a valuable opportunity to meet people, to make good first impressions in a setting that doesn't require business "hardball." They are also a good opportunity to get noticed by people making decisions in your company that you might not come in regular contact with. (She calls this "face time")

Current trends blur the lines between business and social interactions. Companies have relaxed dress codes, have "bring your daughter to work days" and are generally making an attempt to be more social and family-friendly in an increasingly tight labor market. Major business transactions take place on golf courses, at restaurants, or over dinner in private homes. The ability to "socialize" in a business sense is becoming increasingly important. Business parties are one of the venues you can use in your favor, and you shouldn't miss the opportunity.

The choice is yours. Make your decision on whether or not to attend on what you know about the party, your comfort level, and your gut-feel about the circumstances.

*Note-*The administrative staff is often the best source of information. Things that are helpful to know:

Who's Hosting the Party?

It's a good idea to know whose idea the party was, what are their motives? Was it The Boss? The Human Resource Department? The Sales staff? Some parties are intended to enhance the teamwork and camaraderie among their workforce. Some companies have holiday parties for clients, and consider it an important strategic and political performance. Some throw them to impress their vendors and intimidate their competitors. Some companies just throw holiday parties because they think they should. (Everybody else does!)

What Should I Wear?

If in doubt, err on the side of being just a bit more conservative than everyone else. You might want to add something fun-like a Santa Claus tie or red and green socks for a man, or holiday earrings for a woman. This gives you a "conversation piece:" people are bound to comment on it, which can help break the ice. Don't overdo it, though.

Who will Be There?

Flip through your "people file" or contact software before the party to refresh your memory about the people that you know (or should know.) Think of possible topics of conversation in case you end up in the buffet line next to an important client.

How to Make An Entrance?

Pause when you enter, before you start mingling with people. This will give you an opportunity to gauge the atmosphere and adjust your plans accordingly. Is the room loud and raucous, polite and elegant or uncomfortably quiet? Who is in the room? How are they arranged? Are people engaged in small individual conversations or gathered in large groups? Who are the large groups congregated around? Although you may have come with an idea of whom you'd like to see and what you might like to talk about, adjust your plans according to the opportunities that present themselves.

Business/social holiday functions abound. Be sure you take the time to spend time with your family and friends. Being able to provide for and enjoy opportunities with them is a big part of the reasons you're working in the first place!

22. ON GOAL-SETTING

You must have long range goals to keep you from being frustrated by short range failures.

-Charles C. Noble

With the hype about the changing millennium those of us who don't normally succumb to the usual resolution making find ourselves succumbing to the enormity of it all.

The reality that the world is changing hits us even more significantly. If you've seen the retrospective documentaries on TV, heard the sound bytes in Yanni's Auld Lang Syne Mix, or picked up a magazine in the past month, you have been confronted with pictures and analyses of how things have changed and how the pace of change is accelerating.

How can you become part of that change, and make it work for you, rather than simply watching another year go by and being overwhelmed by the fact that you can now get e-mail from a wristwatch?

Set an appropriate focus, and commit to it. This is the single-most important factor in making things happen. A single-minded purpose, with absolute dedication to it, is a powerful thing. It is also a difficult thing. What if you commit to the wrong thing? What if you should have put your time and effort in a new product line rather than improving customer service? Unfortunately, if you fail to commit, or attempt too many things at once, or wait too long to see where the market or your competitors are going before you move, you probably won't do an acceptable job on either your product line or your customer service.

Give initiatives enough time. Don't subscribe to the "flavor of the week" style of management. Figure three weeks to effect a change in yourself (form a new habit or break one) and exponentially longer depending on the number of people and external factors involved.

Remember the importance of motivation. There are things you may be able to change just because you're the boss, but the change will be short-lived and not as effective as you'd like it to be unless you find a way to get everybody else's "heart and soul" into the act. If in doubt about what would motivate people, ask them.

23. On Selective Laziness

There is more to life than increasing its speed.

-Mahatma Gandhi

With the new millennium, many people are resolving to work harder. I'm resolving to be lazier.

There have been times when I've done either of the above and nearly run myself ragged getting myself out of the scrapes I've gotten myself into.

Three big energy savers:

- **Be honest.** How much of the sugarcoating, pussyfooting, and beating around the bush that you do every day is really necessary? Granted, it is necessary to present things in a positive light, and sometimes to filter information for security and other reasons. Most managers we've seen spend more time and energy than necessary putting the correct "spin" on information. If you've lost a customer's order, tell them so, and tell them what you intend to do about it. If you've missed a deadline, come clean and include a plan for making up the time. Don't lie awake nights stewing over it, or working yourself into a frenzy covering for it. We're all human, Murphy is alive and well, and things don't always go according to plan. Don't waste your energy, and more importantly, your credibility, by stretching the truth.

- **Don't agonize over decisions.** If you make your decisions based on the principles that you and your company adhere to, you never have to justify yourself. (or can at least do it much more simply.) Making decisions counter to those principles, even if the reason seemed good at the time (I'll do this for you if you do that for me) or out of real or perceived loyalty to a person or entity, or for any other reason, puts you in a bit of a spot. You spend a lot more energy explaining your decisions and reasoning, rather than simply citing the principle.

- **Avoiding Competing and Getting Even**. We've all felt the inclination to do better than our rivals, or make sure they find out about your successes, especially if they disagreed with you in the past. Unfortunately, the other guy feels the same inclination and will generally try to retaliate. Getting into these escalating competitive situations is best left to the racquetball court or to direct market competition, not to internal one-upmanship, unless it's extremely good-natured and takes place among friends.

It's amazing to see how much work people manufacture for themselves, and how many people burn themselves out unnecessarily on these three points. Next time you feel stressed or overwhelmed, try to step back from what you're doing and look at it from this perspective. How can you tell if you have any of these problems? "Yes" answers to any of the following may indicate that some introspection is necessary:

- Are you afraid to take a vacation?
- Do you feel you have to handle tasks (especially communications) yourself rather than delegating?
- Do you feel inclined to "cover" for your boss to your subordinates, or vice versa?
- Do you scramble to meet customers' inflated expectations? (Or fail to meet them altogether?)
- Do you dread meetings or certain conversations?

- When you write status reports, does it bring back memories of your college classes in creative writing?

- Have you failed (or hesitated) to provide your subordinates clearly defined job descriptions, project plans, etc. that really and truly define your expectations of them?

- Would you object to your boss reviewing these job descriptions, project plans, etc.?

If the answers to any of the above are "yes," you may have some cleanup work to do. Many of these messes we get ourselves into begin very innocently, but gain complexity and impact as time goes on if they're not aired, discussed and resolved frequently.

24. ON LISTENING TO CUSTOMERS

Listen, or your tongue will make you deaf.

-Native American Proverb

The opposite of talking isn't listening. The opposite of talking is waiting.

-Fran Lebowitz

Companies spend a LOT of money on mailing lists, demographic surveys, and electronic data that neatly segments demographics of customers. In contrast, very few companies actually take the time to communicate with customers.

It is absolutely vital to have good, current, accurate information on the demographics of your customers. It is imperative to know who your customers are. You have to know how to reach them, communicate with them, and serve their needs. You have to understand what they like and dislike about your product. Technology can make this easier. Used incorrectly, however, technology just adds another layer between your company and your customers, and that is something you simply cannot afford.

There is no substitute for talking to customers. Customers speak from real experience. Although statistics are valuable, they are only a starting point for theory and generalization. It's amazing to me to watch a roomful of business people standing around charts, graphs, and spreadsheets that are supposed to tell them about their customer demographics. They use expensive software to collect data from their web sites. Many of these marketing execs have probably never spoken to a customer.

They instead spend their time tracking "cookies" collected by their web site and coming up with strategies to issue price club cards to identify their customers and study their buying habits. I even read an article about a lawsuit involving telephone companies "right" to sell telephone records to marketing companies.

Companies that use such services and buy such demographic data argue that they want to be able to provide better service to their customers. The telephone record article used the example of a company that provides funeral services. They may use information about individuals that frequently contact medical providers and suppliers of elderly products to "target" potential customers for their services.

Would a consumer so targeted be grateful that their needs have been anticipated, or angry that their privacy has been violated?

In their enthusiasm to get ahead of their competitors, many companies are employing technological tools that are of dubious value and push ethical limits. The time and money would be better spent coming up with a comprehensive marketing strategy, and using tools judiciously and respectfully to get key information that supports your strategy.

If in doubt about what customers think, don't spy on them. Just ask them!

25. ON SELLING

Half the battle is selling music, not singing it. It's the image, not what you sing.

—Rod Stewart

There is more similarity in the marketing challenge of selling a precious painting by Degas and a frosted mug of root beer than you ever thought possible.

-Alfred Taubman

It's amazing how many executives I've talked to who claim to hate selling. You cannot possibly be an effective executive without being an effective sales person. You have to convince people to support your initiatives, you have to get people to get along with one another, and you have to sell the overall vision of the company you're building. All of these are sales tasks. You can't be truly good at anything you hate.

Believe in What You're Selling

There are very few talented dramatists in the world. And even for people with thespian talent, acting a part that they don't personally believe in takes a lot more energy than one that is more closely aligned with their true selves.

Conviction, passion, and belief are communicated in the way you carry and express yourself. People are consciously and subconsciously drawn to leaders who strongly believe in something, and whose actions are consistent with their words. By the same token, leaders who don't show integrity, consciously and subconsciously repel people. For example, if they exhibit any duplicity or inconsistency between their actions and beliefs, you have a hard time believing what they say.

Develop a Clear Picture

If you can't clearly picture your objective, it is very difficult to get people to buy into it. Simple is good.

Communicate Well

Communicate this picture clearly with everyone associated with it. Customers, clients, co-workers, anyone who will listen should be convinced of what you're trying to do and the value of doing it. Don't leave anyone out-because anyone who doesn't receive an "engraved invitation" to participate in your vision may feel excluded or offended and consequently be more resistant to your ideas.

Be Positive

Be positive about both your idea and the capabilities of people to help you achieve it. People are much more receptive to positive messages than negative ones, so frame your communications in a positive format. "Doing XYZ is achievable by our talented people, and it will give us these advantages..." is much easier to swallow than "We might fail to do XYZ because our staff is already overwhelmed, but if we don't do it, we'll have these problems..." People tend to ignore the negative words in your phrases. When you tell people—"Don't think about pink elephants," they immediately picture pink elephants.

Negative statements, as well as thoughts and feelings, are simply not as effective as positive ones.

As an executive, strategist or manager, you are selling something every day of your life. In order to do that successfully, you need to believe in what you're selling, develop a clear picture, communicate well, and be positive. If you can do those four things, you are a much more effective sales person.

26. On Feeding People

If this is coffee, please bring me some tea; but if this is tea, please bring me some coffee.

-Abraham Lincoln

One of my most powerful memories of a corporate culture was just out of college, working for a small design firm in Bountiful, Utah. The company had worldwide clients, but was very small, and family-based.

Most of the people that worked there (around 30 of us at that office) were very talented but young just out of college, and many were far from home. The inexperience and the creative mix of people could have (and often did) lead to equally powerful personality conflicts. But there was one thing that held us all together. – Food!

Most Fridays during the summer, we had a cookout. Friday was dress-down day, so we were all wearing jeans, anyway.

We would spend about two hours (between setup and cleanup) working together, swatting flies, looking for the lost pepper, celebrating the week's accomplishments, and sharing stories about our kids' little league experiences, challenges with in-laws, personal tragedies, jury duty, who was dating whom, and the merits of various clothing stores.

A catering company handled some of the details, but the owner himself (normally in pinstripes, now in a checkered apron) manned the barbecue and personally served every one of us. We usually had hamburgers and hot dogs, but once he brought salmon from his fishing trip to Alaska and made sure we all had some.

Expensive? Yes. Inefficient? Very. Messy? Absolutely. But it also contributed heavily to building a team that was determined to handle just about anything the owner threw at us.

27. On Finding the Balance Point

Everybody knows if you are too careful, you are so occupied in being careful that you are sure to stumble over something.

-Gertrude Stein

Listening to an old interview with the late martial arts master Bruce Lee, I was struck by a line of discussion that he took when talking about why he was so successful.

There were, at the time, two schools of thought about martial arts-one was rigid forms, practice, and discipline. The other was fluid, instinctive "street fighting."

Lee felt that the ideal to strive for was the perfect balance point between the two-between discipline and instinct.

I think that in management and business, there is also a "balance point."

On one extreme, you have discipline. The late nights you spend studying for your MBA or CPA. The required early morning staff meetings. Your charts, graphs, statistics and reports, diligently studied, annotated, dog-eared and flagged.

On the other extreme, you have your gut feelings about people and situations, the great idea that wakes you up in the middle of the night. The chance conversation at the grocery store that seems somehow relevant to a problem you're dealing with. The "idea file" you keep in your bottom drawer.

Neither extreme alone will get you where you want to go. If discipline and hard work is your sole advantage, the next person who comes along will outclass you. He or she will have more energy or fewer distractions (read relationships, kids, hobbies, a "life") and could be imitated by anyone.

If creativity and instinct are your only strong suits, you'll never see an idea live long enough to be fully implemented. You have to have the practicality, homework and diligence to see it through.

Although Bruce Lee was not an executive, I think he certainly would have been good at it because he cultivated both creativity and instinct. When he competed, you could see him visibly relax and call upon his instincts to know the next move. When he moved, however, his motions were polished by years of training.

He demonstrated the power of seeking the balance point.

28. On Getting Out of the Way!

The pleasure of criticizing robs us of the pleasure of being moved by some very fine things.

Jean de La Bruyère

"I can't believe they hired a consultant to find a solution before they even asked us what the problem was!"

"They paid a headhunter an obscene amount of money when I could have just e-mailed an acquaintance who was perfect for this job!" They spent all that money on putting the plan and sales pitch together, and that plan was based on the "yellow sticky note" metaphor but they didn't take into account the fact that the client hates yellow sticky notes. I knew that from working with him!"

Your people are skilled and qualified, they know the company, and they know the clients. So why do you sweat in silence over problems, or hire outsiders to do simple jobs, instead of getting out of the way and letting your own people help the company succeed?

There is a fine line between outsourcing a short-term or specialized piece of work (which is often a good strategy) and overlooking your resident talent when solving a problem.

Deloitte & Touche leverages its internal resources with a Refer Potential Movers & Shakers (RPMs for short) as its "single best source of high-talent hires." Employees receive $1,500 to $10,000 (depending on the position) for referrals that result in filling positions from a list that is e-mailed weekly to everyone. Referring employees are also entered in drawings for a Jeep or Blazer (out of deference to clients Daimler/Chrysler and General Motors.)

They have paid out a total of $3.5 million to employees in cash and prizes since 1998. They would have paid more than $10 million in traditional recruiting methods to fill the same 1,200 positions.

Zions Bank in Salt Lake City pays referral fees to any employee that refers a new client; the amount of the fee is commensurate with the amount and type of the client relationship.

Any company, large or small, can do the same thing. The steps are always the same. The means of doing them will vary, depending on the type of company and nature of the situation.

- Communicate issues and goals.
- Solicit contributions objectively.
- Measure results (in increased earnings or savings.)
- Reward accordingly (a percentage of the amount earned or saved.)

The benefits to leveraging your internal talent are many:

- You generally save money over outside sources.
- You get better, more specific, more tailored solutions to real problems.
- You keep confidential information limited to a smaller group (when you hire an outside firm, be sure to have confidentiality agreements, etc.)
- You increase job satisfaction among your current people by adding variety.
- You make them feel valued and listened to.

People have a remarkable capacity to exceed your expectations, if you tell them what the objectives are, then get out of the way and let them help achieve them!

29. On Detail

God is in the details.

-Mies van der Rohe

Many times a grand, sweeping, epic idea is killed by a detail, or the lack thereof. Imagine a huge, beautiful, 8-layered wedding cake-the cake is moist, perfect and spongy; the icing pure white; the decorations elegant, the lighting on the cake making it a striking centerpiece on a dramatic reception table.

Now imagine a fly stuck in the icing on the third layer from the top.

You can see how a lot of creative thought and hard work can be ruined by a tiny oversight.

You can imagine a brilliant project plan with a misspelling in it, a wonderful new home with a broken light fixture, a handsome man in a well-tailored suit with polished shoes and spinach in his teeth, a mint-perfect new car that smells like fish, or a wonderful dinner served without a fork.

That being said, it requires diligence, organization, and observation to take care of all the details. Here are methods we've used with success-pick the ones that work best for the situation:

- Check things from all angles, especially before you hand something in to your boss or hand it over to the customer.

- Use technology wherever you can. There is software that will check your spelling, do your math for you (or at least double-check it) or help you draw perfect circles and squares that are exactly the right size and line them up precisely.

- Have someone check your work. A second set of eyes will catch things you've looked at over and over again and not seen. The "buddy system" is good for this, especially if you pair up with someone with a good eye for detail in areas you may miss. Promise to be ruthless to one another-it's for your own good!

- Use "Planner" tools to capture details to be checked or otherwise resolved—Use a notebook, calendar, personal planner or tiny computer to write down and check off details for yourself and people to whom you delegate.

- A whiteboard-Write down anything relevant that needs to be captured, together with the name of the person responsible to take care of it and the date. Keep this in your meeting room or a common area.

- Meeting minutes-Take notes (or get a copy of someone else's) in every meeting you attend, and check off the "action items" for the next meeting throughout the week as you do them.

- Gantt Charts-For large, complicated projects, this is the best way to keep track of a large number of interdependent tasks, schedules, costs, etc. Many of these also tell you when you've assigned too much to a particular person that occurs at the same time.

- Phone messages-One manager I know will call her own voice mail at work when something occurs to her over the weekend. This way she remembers the detail when she gets to work.

- E-mail-You can schedule e-mails to be sent to people (or yourself!) to remind them of specific tasks at specific times.

- Be prepared for emergencies. It doesn't take much time, money or space to have an extra printer cartridge, an extra copy of a document, a safety pin or a toothbrush in your desk or briefcase.

There is a fine line between being a perfectionist and being obsessive. Give some thought to employing these ideas to pay attention to the details. Bring your standards of quality up a notch, and you'll often find that it takes very little effort to make all the difference in your success.

30. ON SMALL GIFTS

It is always so pleasant to be generous, though very vexatious to pay debts.

-Ralph Waldo Emerson

Imagine finding a pair of movie passes in a plain envelope on your chair. You wonder who they're from and for what reason. You wonder if your coworkers have received them, and if so, if it was the whole team, the whole department, or just those deemed as "top performers" by the team lead, department head, or some other mysterious entity. You hesitate to ask your co-workers because they might feel left out if they didn't receive them also.

Now imagine your team (or you) being personally presented with that same set of movie tickets by the CEO of the company, along with a round of applause from your peers, in recognition of a specific achievement your team (or you personally) worked very hard on.

Big difference? Absolutely. It takes a bit more planning but usually doesn't cost any more to make those little gifts and tokens of appreciation exponentially more meaningful.

Here are some ideas-

- Always be specific about the reason. Even if it's just a "you've been putting in a lot of hours lately to deal with the new computer system."

- Let people know who else is receiving the gift and why-half of the fun is sharing the joy with others. If you announce (or indicate in a card) that it was the team or department, or the top 10% performers on the sales staff (with names) that gives the receivers tacit permission to talk to one another and enjoy the moment together.

- Make awards publicly if possible. Recognition can mean more than the gift itself, especially if it leads to other opportunities for that person.

- Leave a note the person can save. Use fancy cards or certificates whenever possible. Most desktop publishing software allows you to create or embellish a card, certificate or even a simple sheet of paper with clipart, borders, and other decoration. We see many of these hanging on walls in cubicles later, or tucked away in a "brag file" for that person's next performance evaluation that allows them to draw attention their accomplishments.

- Have the gift presented by, (or at least have the note signed by,) the highest-ranking person in the company you can find. This assures the person that their efforts are getting noticed in more than just their immediate circle.

- Even if a gift is a surprise, or you don't want to identify yourself as the giver, make something up so that you can at least give them the reason for the gift and identify the other recipients.

"The Easter Bunny has noticed how hard your team has been working to get this merger accomplished." Or "A little bird brought your work on Project X to the attention of the CEO."

It's been our experience that twenty bucks on an inexpensive gift or token can pay for itself exponentially in morale and performance.

You can maximize that investment of twenty bucks to another degree of magnitude by simply giving some thought to the manner of giving.

31. On Abundance

The world is full of abundance and opportunity, but far too many people come to the fountain of life with a sieve instead of a tank car, or a teaspoon instead of a steam shovel. They expect little and as a result they get little.

-Ben Sweetland

It used to be that rare things were valuable. If diamonds were there on the ground for anyone to pick up, they wouldn't be as valuable as they are.

There is another side to that theory, however. Some things are more valuable because of their abundance!

Take the fax machine. The first one produced was absolutely useless, because there was no one to fax *to*. The more common fax machines become, the more it becomes a necessity to have one in order to do business. Suddenly customers expect to be able to fax you orders, and your suppliers can serve you faster if you fax your orders to them.

The same is true of success in business. It's true there can be only one "top dog," and most organizational charts have fewer squares the higher up the page you look, up to a single CEO. But there are more and more companies to become CEO of. As companies get larger, there are more and more management spots opening up than can easily be filled. And the management positions are offering more flexibility, responsibility and creativity. And they're paying more.

Self-directed teams, succession planning, and many other new management insights call for a paradigm shift- business is no longer dog-eat-dog competitive. There are people who have proven that the more people you help succeed, the more successful you become yourself. Emerson said "invention breeds invention." We propose that "success breeds success."

32. On Your Worst Client as Your Best Friend

He that wrestles with us strengthens our nerves and sharpens our skill. Our antagonist is our helper.

        -Edmund Burke

We have met the enemy and it is us.

        -Walt Kelly, "Pogo" comic strip

We should ever conduct ourselves toward our enemy as if he were one day to be our friend.

        -John Henry Newman

Nobody likes whiners. Especially when you've worked hard to produce results for a customer, and feel sure that you've exceeded every possible expectation-and then they rain on your parade by finding fault with a detail you feel is less relevant than YOU think it is.

Granted, there are some people you just can't please, but it always pays to listen.

"I was really angry after the phone call, but two weeks later, I was really happy about the changes we've made." A program director for a radio station told me.

"I used to spend hours doing research and preparing games for the morning show. Then I get this call from a listener telling us to just lighten up, play more music, and not try to make people THINK in the morning. I was furious." Having invested a lot of time and energy in preparing clever, well thought-out material, the comment sounded unappreciative, to say the least.

After giving the matter some thought, the program director made a few changes to format. Listenership went up, the amount of time she spent preparing the morning show went down, and everybody won. Our program director started receiving more positive phone calls about the format of the show.

"The customer isn't always right, but the customer is always the customer." Unfortunately, when you have several customers to deal with, you have to pick and choose the grains of truth, sometimes from the middle of the most irritating encounters.

A call center manager gave us some tips on dealing with negative comments:

- Sometimes the best defense is no defense. Don't start defending yourself, your product or your company until you've listened to the customer long enough to hear everything that might contain useful information. This will usually give them a chance to unwind enough to be in a more receptive mood to listen to alternatives.

- Be creative in finding solutions to the customer's problem. Engage the customer in that process and ask him or her what he or she would suggest as a solution. Sometimes you get great ideas this way. "This is the critical point where you find out whether feedback is actually useful or just somebody having a bad day."

- Always forward, don't filter. Send comments to the department or manager you think is most capable of addressing the issue. Send the whole thing, no matter how offensive you may find it personally. You never know which parts may be useful, and the decision-makers need to understand the strength of the customer's feelings. Professional people don't need to be sheltered.

- Everything from the clever cup holders in your car, to the fact that Levi's Jeans have rivets where they're supposed to be (and none where they're not supposed to be,) microwaveable TV dinners, and e-mail are all the results of customers not being complacent with what exists, and bringing those discontents to the ears of those who can fix them.

Welcome the whines. Or at least, listen to them!

33. On Being Specific

I have always wanted to be somebody, but I see now I should have been more specific.

-Lily Tomlin

We've heard "Be careful what you wish for. You might get it!"

A lesser-known version- "Be careful what you ask for. You might get it!"

You write on a request for candidates to the HR department-"We're looking for a professional." You get a string of applicants who are well dressed, have nice teeth, and a large vocabulary. They also know absolutely nothing about your business or the role they would be expected to play in it.

A report you've turned in comes back with a yellow sticky note that says, "This is good stuff, but it wasn't exactly what I was looking for." You're left wondering whether it's the topic, the angle, the depth, or the font that he doesn't like.

We're convinced that 80% of the difficulties and frustrations in the business world result from incomplete or inaccurate communication- Most people try very hard to do their jobs, to meet the expectations of their clients and co-workers, and to be valued and appreciated.

That's almost impossible to do when solid, specific information either wasn't communicated, or wasn't received. Here are some ways we've come across to ensure specific communication:

- Write everything down. Written policies, procedures, agreements, and specifications make it much easier to have a solid understanding during and after the discussion. Use drawings, tables, anything that helps get your meaning across.

- Use examples. Even a bad example, showing a report that doesn't meet your needs, and explaining what you need done differently, is better than having people fly blind.

- Ask questions, and welcome questions when they're asked of you.

- Use lots of adjectives. Describe what you expect in detail.

- Explain any experiences you've had that didn't meet your expectations. Admit to mistakes you've made in the past so that other people don't repeat them.

- Be specific with positive feedback, as well as negative. "I really like the way you handled the finances in this document. The graphs make things very easy to follow."

- You may not know the particulars of how something is accomplished, especially when you're managing highly skilled specialists. Be specific about the requirements of the end result, even if you leave the particulars about HOW to accomplish it up to them. Be sure you communicate well enough to understand the requirements and the options of how to achieve them, even if you don't know the mechanics of how it's done.

Communicating specific expectations is probably the most important (and difficult) step in achieving what you want or need to happen. Spending some extra time on this factor is well worth it.

34. On Expectations

Everyone believes very easily whatever they fear or desire.

-Jean de la Fontaine

They can because they think they can.

-Virgil

Several years ago, I had to give a presentation to a group of bankers in Nevada. I did not know any of them, and had never given a presentation to so many high-ranking executives.

Most of my teammates were more experienced and considered me a bit too green to be giving so important a presentation by myself.

My senior team member that accompanied me on the trip told me- "You're the authority on Year 2000 issues. You're going to have to be in absolute control for the first half-hour, or they won't have the information they need to make the rest of the day productive." I think my teammate was prepared to jump in at the first sign of waffling on my part.

I was nervous. I had practiced until I knew the presentation cold. I was prepared for any question. I was doing relaxation exercises. I was practically chanting mantras on the plane trip over. But once I got up in front of this group, I opened with a joke but then got right down to business. My teammate relaxed after the first slide. "You really controlled the room. And you did it your way-not the way you were told, but it was even more effective that way."

The reason it was so easy, I told him, was because the people who expected me to fail were hundreds of miles away. The people I was presenting to didn't know me, so I was able to completely forget myself and become immersed in the material. I didn't worry about what they would think because I didn't have the inertia of their negative expectations.

Years later, a couple of people on my team were preparing to give a presentation to a group of peers and superiors (mostly superiors.) "They aren't the 'public speaking' type." I had been told repeatedly. But they were the most educated on the topic, and learning the public speaking was something that would be very useful to their professional development.

We worked on the presentation for weeks, and they were convinced that they could do it with polish. We had a couple of rehearsals, in which they were brilliant.

The day of the presentation, however, they lost some of their brilliance in front of the crowd. They hemmed and hawed a bit, shuffled through notes, and were substantially less inspired than intimidated. They were both disappointed with their performance.

"They were expecting us to screw up." One told me. "It's like the gravitational pull of their opinions was just too much to overcome."

Why is it that the expectations of the audience (not just for public speaking, but with the performance of any task or skill) have so much to do with the outcome? And what can we do to turn this phenomenon into an advantage, rather than a disadvantage?

- Many career advisors recommend changing jobs every two years or so. This is not just because you've outgrown your current position, but also because you may have outgrown your colleague's expectations. Getting a fresh start with a new "crowd" can help raise the bar by having everyone's expectations set higher to begin with than with a group of people who remember you as being green out of school, or new in the industry.

- You can get the same benefit by finding new opportunities at your present job, being the interface with a new department, or by finding a new client or group of clients to interact with.

- Speak well of your employees. (When you're speaking to them directly, or speaking to others about them.) When sending people to do a sales presentation, rather than saying "Since Michael is too green to be doing this himself, I'm also sending Lisa," say "I'm sending Lisa along on this trip because she's spent some time with this client and may have some suggestions." Wording things positively takes some practice but it makes a huge difference in the outcome.

- Find new (hopefully appreciative) audiences for your people.

- Be very careful how you phrase expectations of yourself. Rather than saying: "I can't do that report by myself," say "I'll need some help with this specific section."

- Be as private as possible with criticism. "I would have preferred that you handle this situation in a different way," is a conversation that should take place at a private table over lunch, or behind a closed office door.

- Be as public as practical with positive feedback. "Thanks to some quick thinking by Lee, we were able to exploit an opportunity we might have missed." Will go over well in a sales meeting, or a status report to the top brass.

People's capacity to meet your expectations (whether they be good or bad) is amazing. That capacity is constantly at play, whether your realize it or not.

The danger is that if you're not consciously aware of it, you may lapse into setting negative expectations without meaning to.

Before I gave my presentation to the Nevada bankers, my teammates all had my best interests at heart. They didn't realize (nor did I) that I had to escape their negative expectations to have the opportunity to shine.

The good news is that by being aware of the power of expectation, you can create opportunities for yourself and your people to shine without ever leaving town.

35. How **NOT** to handle a Merger or Acquisition

Reorganizing can be a wonderful method for creating the illusion of progress while producing confusion, inefficiency, and demoralization.
                                                        -Petronius Arbiter

Note: Sometimes the best way to express a concept is by sarcasm. In case you missed it, this essay is tongue in cheek.

- Don't communicate with employees. If you ignore them, they'll go away. With any luck, they'll even start their own company with your products and processes, and do them better, faster and cheaper than you ever could. By the time you're done being distracted by this merger business you'll never know what hit you. But with competition that good, you'll never have to worry about an anti-trust lawsuit!

- Don't communicate with the public. They'll find out about the deal through the newspapers. Editorial columnists are much better communicators than anyone from your company, and best of all, you don't have to pay them!

- Don't communicate with your customers. They'll find out when they see a new name on their invoices and wonder what the heck happened. You'll be free from the pesky ties of customer loyalty forever.

- Don't communicate with your shareholders. Now that they're just a fraction of a larger pool of constituents you have to worry about, you might as well ignore them.

- Do things exactly the way you always have. Now that you have two accounting departments, two human resource departments, two communication departments, etc., you can play them against one another; or assign the same tasks to both and see who does them better.

- Handle layoffs as publicly as possible. Hold a mandatory meeting in the auditorium, with lots of obvious security hanging around. Announce the names of employees to be laid off, and have them escorted by security to gather their belongings and exit the building. It's much more efficient that way. This method has the added benefit of scaring your remaining employees into submission. Make sure each department manager is as territorial and possessive as possible. Circulate rumors. If they don't know what you do, they can't take you over!

36. On Bamboo Trees

There's an Asian parable about an oak tree and a bamboo. The oak tree appears to be larger and stronger, but in a typhoon, it will be broken to splinters. The bamboo, on the other hand, will bend with the wind and spring back as strong as ever.

The climate in the business world has gotten much windier in recent years.

We've gotten a lot of comments on the advice to change jobs every two years or so.

- "Whatever happened to company loyalty?"
- "How can you get really good at something if you're jumping around so much?"
- "Don't you get attached to people and projects?"

Of course, every person's temperament and situation is different. There are some very successful "lifers" who grow with their company and stay with it for 20 or 30 years or even more.

The point we need to clarify is this; if you want to progress in your job, your skills, and your contacts, you really should make major changes to your roles and responsibilities at least every two years. You can very successfully do this at the same company. The company wins by having a better, more well informed employee.

- Get yourself assigned to different client accounts. You'll learn new ways of doing things.
- Work for a different department affiliated with the one you work for now. You'll get a better perspective of how the company is put together.
- Start a new project.
- Learn a new skill.

- Make new acquaintances and alliances.
- Even redecorating your workspace will help you shake some of the dust off and see things differently.

If you do something long enough that you feel you could do it in your sleep, you've been there too long. There are too many people who are "retired on the job." Once you get yourself dug in to far and too heavily invested in one skill, company, department or profession, you become resistant to change because it's no longer comfortable for you.

Like it or not, change is more prevalent and more rapid than ever. Technology, economic changes, and corporate restructuring all mean that you will undoubtedly do things differently six months from today than you do now.

Digging your roots in deep and building solid skills and experience is important. Being flexible enough to adapt to change can be equally, or even more important.

37. BEWARE OF EXPERTS

Many highly intelligent people are poor thinkers. Many people of average intelligence are skilled thinkers. The power of a car is separate from the way the car is driven.

-Edward De Bono

The most likely way for the world to be destroyed, most experts agree, is by accident. That's where we come in; we're computer professionals. We cause accidents.

-Nathaniel Borenstein

An expert is one who knows more and more about less and less.

-Nicholas Murray Butler

The vast majority of consulting professionals are highly ethical, helpful people. There is a small minority of "experts" in nearly every field that are hazardous to your business' health. These people give the rest of consulting a bad name, which is unfortunate-for the consulting industry; and for you, as the business owner or manager.

It is inefficient and unreasonable for most businesses to employ an expert in every field that ever touches that business. Having a world-class department in such varied fields as accounting, HR, technology, and law, as well as experts in whatever product or service your company specializes in would be a luxury. Even the largest companies can't (or would rather not) afford all of these experts. Depending on how often they need those specific areas of expertise, hiring a consultant for occasional, limited or special circumstances makes perfect sense.

Unfortunately, there are those that are not only expensive and useless to your company; but actually harmful because of the havoc they wreak with your budget, your decision-making processes, and your competitors. This article isn't long enough for examples, but there are plenty in three excellent books on the topic-

- *The Witch Doctors: Making Sense of the Management Gurus*
- *Dangerous Company: Management Consultants and the Businesses They Save and Ruin*
- *Consulting Demons: Inside the Unscrupulous World of Global Corporate Consulting*

Things to watch out for:

- Single point of entry-Do you ever get to talk to anyone at that company besides the account representative? Do you feel like you are discouraged from direct communication with other people at that company? (Or that they are discouraged from talking to you without filtering everything through the account rep?) A good rep's job is to act as a facilitator, not a barrier.

- Lack of references-They may indicate that their client relationships are confidential, and therefore they can't give you references. If they've done a good job for other companies, however, they should be able to obtain permission from previous clients to give you selected information about how they have helped their clients. NO references generally mean that their previous clients either had poor experiences, or that there were no previous clients with situations remotely similar.

- Lack of credentials-Are their certifications from anywhere you've ever heard of? These are easier to check now than ever before, because most accredited learning institutions have web sites indicating something about their size and specialty. Few people check credentials, however. Make sure you're getting the skills that were represented, and not a student or junior-level person who is learning the necessary skills while billing time to your company.

- Foot-in-the-Door syndrome-Is the consultant trying to get you dependent on a system or setup that your current staff does not have the skills to run on a day-to-day basis? This could make the consulting firm indispensable for ongoing support and training.

- If you're planning major changes or system conversions, it's fine to have a consulting company help with the startup until your team gets staffed and trained. Make sure it is a decision you've thought through and are prepared to invest in, and not a "seeding" process to hook your company into a relationship much longer than the initial project was anticipated to be. Make sure that there is a specific end-date that everyone agrees to, and the terms of that engagement will leave you self-sufficient by that end-date.

- Confidentiality agreements. Agree to provide positive references to help the consulting firm with their marketing efforts. That's only fair, but be sure to specify what information they can provide, and under what circumstances. You don't want them helping your competitors with information they learned while working with you.

Many companies have "strategic relationships" with several consulting or outsourcing firms. By doing this, they can concentrate on their own product or service, keep their employment expenses low, and take advantage of economies of scale by paying for what they need when they need it. Consultants get very good at their specialty as they serve a number of different companies-they also have the advantage of being a large specialized firm-they can afford training and equipment that a smaller department couldn't.

It's a great arrangement for both sides, as long as everyone maintains good communication, and takes these few basic precautions.

38. On Making it Up as you Go

You can't get there by bus, only by hard work and risk and by not quite knowing what you're doing. What you'll discover will be wonderful. What you'll discover will be yourself.

-Alan Alda

It's always a good idea to do some research, have some case studies and role models to help you make decisions. Unfortunately (Or fortunately, for those of us who like uncharted territory!) there are many situations for which there are no precedents. New technology, new market forces, and other factors create a lot of options that have never existed before. So what do you do when there's no one to ask?

There are a lot of project methodologies available from a number of sources. We like the PMI model available from the Project Management Institute for the following reasons-1) it works, 2) it provides a common vocabulary and set of tools for communicating about projects, and 3) it offers a certification program.

Following a methodology is very important for projects to succeed. More important than that, however, is to decide what projects to pursue, and why!

Step 1—Ask "Why" Questions

Many people jump too quickly to what they think needs to be done, rather than exploring "why" they're doing things in the first place. A small team "bucked the system" at Burlington Northern (the transportation company) when the rest of the company was promoting the standard freight car service. This small group advocated letting the standard freight cars rot, and devoting resources instead to the "piggyback" flat bed cars. (These carry trailers ready for over-the-road trucks to hitch up and drive off without unloading the cars.)

The piggyback service is now a major component of Burlington Northern's success.

Step 2—Develop a Broad Objective

In the Burlington Northern example, defining a broader objective (to capture transportation market share) worked much more effectively than the narrower objective of pursuing a larger percentage of the standard freight car market. Broader objectives give you more options.

Step 3—Develop an Action Plan (Project Plan)

Take your broad objective and brainstorm ways to achieve it. Research the most likely possibilities, using objective criteria to choose among them. Consider everything, no matter how far-fetched. The only ideas you should discard out of hand are those that violate ethical principles. (This is where you start a project methodology.)

Step 4—Manage Risk

Figure out what could go wrong, and what you could do to reduce the likelihood of bad things happening, or the severity if it does happen.

Step 5—Communicate To All Stakeholders

Explain what you're doing and why, and when you will start. Never surprise your stakeholders, (except maybe by succeeding when they think you won't!)

Step 6—Do it!

Too many people wait around for permission, or wait for someone else to take responsibility for their actions. At best, they find that others are always taking credit for their successes when they do happen.

At worst, they end up sitting around forever and are seen as unproductive.

If you take the responsibility yourself, you risk failure, but if you're following a good methodology and have done your homework on step #4, (managing risk) the risk is slim.

"Until one is committed there is hesitancy,
the chance to draw back, always ineffectiveness.
"Concerning all acts of initiative (and creation)
there is one elementary truth
the ignorance of which kills countless ideas and
splendid plans
that the moment one definitely commits oneself,
then Providence moves too.
"All sorts of things occur to help one that would never
otherwise have occurred.
"A whole stream of events issues from the decision,
raising in one's favour all manner of unforeseen
incidents and meetings and material assistance
Which no man could have dreamt would come his way.
I learned a deep respect for one of Goethe's couplets-
'Whatever you can do, or dream you can, begin it.
Boldness has genius, power, and magic in it.'"

-W.H. Murray
From the Scottish Himalayan Expedition

39. ON BRICK WALLS

Men build too many walls and not enough bridges.
                                                    -Sir Isaac Newton

People used to set a lot more store by things that appear to be permanent structures than they do now.

"Beating your head against a brick wall" was an expression for doing something with absolutely no possibility of success, because of a barrier. The barrier could be psychological, political, cultural, or even physical.

Just using the example of last 10 years in Europe-the "brick wall" between East and West Germany was followed by attempts at a unified currency and other trade measures of the European Union, followed (according to recent headlines) by the current effort to create unified e-commerce policies between the E.U. and the United States.

If you apply this model to your company, you've probably seen communications improve between departments that were impenetrable silos and empires. You may have even seen more seamless interaction between your own company, your vendor companies and your client companies. Rather than sending a letter or showing up, briefcase in hand, in the lobby; you access their inventory and status information though a web-based interface that fetches the data directly from their databases.

In the midst of all this change and free-flowing information among nations, governments, companies, and departments, you have to wonder.

Are there brick walls in your company that need to come down?

40. On Things You Can Ignore

Allowing an unimportant mistake to pass without comment is a wonderful social grace.

-Judith Martin

The art of being wise is the art of knowing what to overlook.

-William James

With all of the essays we've run lately on things that managers should pay more attention to, we thought it would be refreshing to run an essay on things you can afford to ignore.

Every activity your company engages in can be classified as either "core" or "hygiene." Core activities are those things that make your business different from your competitors. Looking at two pizza companies, for example: Round Table Pizza differentiates itself based on its quality and ingredients. Chuck E. Cheeses differentiates itself on entertainment value. So for Round Table, the pizza itself is core. For Chuck E Cheese, the pizza itself is incidental.

In Living on the Fault Line: Managing for Shareholder Value in the Age of the Internet By Geoffrey A. Moore, Moore indicates that startup companies spend about 80 percent of their people's time and energy on "core" activities, and 20 percent on "hygiene." The more established a company gets, on the other hand, the more time they spend on "hygiene," and the less on "core" activities. The average Fortune 500 inverts that ratio and spends only 20 percent of its time on core activities.

Moore describes hygiene, or context tasks, this way-"Hygiene refers to all the things that the marketplace expects you to do well but gives you no credit for doing exceptionally well. Do you bathe regularly? Good. If you didn't, someone might have to speak to you. But even if you bathe constantly, no one is going to give you a promotion. The same goes for companies that ship what the customer asked for, send a bill that actually corresponds to what was ordered and received, and answer the phone when a customer calls for support. If companies fail to do these things, they will be in trouble, but once they achieve a certain level of consistency in them, they get no premium for doing them better than that."

Given that you have a limited amount of time and energy to spend, you may want to take a hard look the percentages of time you spend on basic company hygiene. If it seems excessive, then delegate, outsource, or just plain ignore it.

Round Table Pizza isn't going to improve its stock price by hiring personnel with theatrical abilities. Their customers don't want to be served by singing bears. By the same token, Chuck E Cheese's is not going to improve its shareholder value by making pizza with sun-dried tomatoes and smoked Gouda. The seven-year-olds at a birthday party probably don't taste the pizza anyway.

These are exaggerated examples, but I'm sure you won't have to look to far to find exorbitant amounts of time and energy being spent on factors that don't matter to your customers or the bottom line.

41. ON PERFORMANCE REVIEWS

An empowered organization is one in which individuals have the knowledge, skill, desire, and opportunity to personally succeed in a way that leads to collective organizational success.

Stephen R. Covey

An employee we'll call "Jane" came out of a performance review furious. She's worked her tail off for the past six months. She had done everything she had thought was expected of her and more; and she had been rewarded with an "acceptable" rating.

Her manager hadn't given it a second thought.

Everybody got "acceptable" ratings, except those who had done something unbelievably good (no one ever had) or indisputably bad (people sometimes did) which would bring their ratings up or down. To the manager, performance reviews were just another paperwork exercise he had to get through every six months-something that took him away from the important business of serving customers and getting things done.

Meanwhile, Jane thinks her accomplishments are ignored and that she's being treated unjustly. Instead of devoting the few minutes before her next meeting to fine-tuning the client presentation she's been putting together, she'll spend the time surfing the web for job opportunities.

Jane's boss never saw her reaction to the review. (Jane's got the poker face down cold) and never asked for Jane's input. And if he had, Jane would have been too upset to speak without an "unprofessional" display of anger, so she would have said something innocuous just to get through the experience and get out of that office before she exploded.

If the manager is disappointed with the difference in Jane's morale and performance—especially on the client presentation she's supposed to be working on now—he will probably have forgotten it by the time the next review rolls around. (Or, just as likely, Jane will have moved on to another employer with whom she feels like she knows where she stands.)

How could this be handled better?

- Make sure the expectations are outlined for everyone's work.

- Document (and make sure each employee agrees to) a set of criteria for "unacceptable" "acceptable" and "exceptional" work, so that everyone knows what the definitions are.

- Ask for employee input a certain amount of time before their review. (And make it clear that you expect their participation! Many people are reluctant to "blow their own horn" unless you insist.)

- Encourage employees to keep a file of examples of exceptional work-problems solved, compliments from customers, projects completed, performance statistics, etc.

- Anything of large impact, or that may be a surprise to the employee, should be handled immediately and not held for a performance review. (Such as blatantly unacceptable performance, adverse customer interactions, etc.)

- After the review, give everyone a chance to mull it over for a few days, then finalize the review by having all parties sign it before it goes into the employee's personnel file.

42. ON BORING JOBS

A wise man will make more opportunities than he finds.

-Francis Bacon

Almost all of us, occasionally, find ourselves in a job that is not as meaningful as we'd like it to be, or find that a job that we DO like comes with some duties that we don't particularly care for. It takes a special kind of person to turn those jobs and those duties into real opportunities.

I know a single mom who is a waitress-not necessarily because she had any particular calling to food service, but because that job suited the hours while her kids were in school. But this young lady is a real artist. She finds meaning in her job by finding ways to make it more than what it is-she doesn't just take orders and carry food, although that is certainly part of it. She orchestrates the patron's experience.

When you're having a business meeting, she unobtrusively clears away the plates and brings more coffee at just the right time to set the tone for business. When a couple is dining out, she subtly adjusts the lighting to enhance the romantic mood.

When a traveling businessperson is dining alone, she chats a bit, suggests the best routes through road construction and offers suggestions on sights to see while in town.

Being able to seize these opportunities not only makes her job more enjoyable and interesting than fetching the next plate of scrambled eggs, it also opens doors to more responsibilities and better opportunities.

Perceptive business people (who belong to your company, or who are clients, or whom you meet in other ways) are always looking for bright, ambitious folks and sooner or later, will notice your extra effort.

This young lady has recently joined the restaurant's management team, and it wouldn't surprise me to see her climb quickly. She might just as easily have met someone wanting to start a catering company, or a businessperson needing a detail-oriented office manager or event planner.

I once had a job doing entry-level graphic art for advertising that involved color separations and paste-ups for an old printing process. It was tedious, repetitive work. The production staff would amuse themselves by having races to see who could prepare an ad, column, or page faster. (The quality control had to be perfect or you'd be disqualified.) The winner of each "race" would get to pick from the remaining work to be done and define the terms of the next contest.

A young man named Greg started work in a large call center and went from entry-level customer service rep with a phone in his ear all day long to trainer to project manager, all within two short years by finding ways of helping people new to the job.

Any job or task can become much more fun and meaningful when you bring a sense of fun and a drive for improvement to it. It's a win-win for companies and managers because the more people enjoy what they're doing, the better at it they generally get.

Customers will enjoy dealing with upbeat, positive folks. Managers can encourage this type of inspiration by being enthusiastic and open-minded.

43. On ROI (Return On Investment)

If you don't have a Masters' degree in finance or accounting, you might find ROI calculations to be a bit intimidating. You may have even put off a project that you know would be valuable just because of the rather daunting task of figuring out how quickly it will pay for itself.

We'll start with an elementary example. Unfortunately, many people jump right into a project based on a feeling that it will be beneficial, but without having actually done the calculation even if they know how the basics of how to calculate ROI. This is unfortunate because then you never really know if your project was successful, and even if you think it was, you couldn't prove it.

Surprisingly, although the actual calculation is the part most people skip-it's also the easiest to actually get done.

The most difficult part is collecting the information you need before you start the project, but you'd need that anyway, even if you weren't calculating ROI.

It goes without saying that any formula is only as good as the numbers that go into it. You need to know:

1) What your current benchmarks are

2) How much the project will actually cost

3) What benefit (or savings) the project will provide

Always start with a benchmark of where you are now. How much are you spending to do the thing that you're planning to automate or improve? For example, if you're spending $2.00 per customer service call for simple inquires, and think you can cut the time your reps spend on those calls by 25% by making the most common information easier to get to (on an intranet, for example) you can save $.50 per call.

You then multiply that by the number of calls per month-if your call center takes 10,000 calls per month, you can save $5000 per month.

So it would take you 2 months to pay for a $10,000 technology implementation.

Your numbers probably won't be quite so simple and round, but starting with this formula will help you do two things-1) communicate to your board why it's a good investment, and 2) measure the success of the project afterward to see if you could do what you said you would.

As a person who hates spreadsheets full of numbers, (and I know I'm not the only one!) I usually put the ROI calculations into some nice, visually attractive charts so that everyone can understand it, whether or not they carry a calculator. It's easy enough to do these days on a reasonably well-equipped PC. A sense of flair or showmanship may be necessary to capture the attention of very busy decision-makers but it's a fine line between drama and credibility.

There is really relatively little math involved-it doesn't take two pots of coffee and a dozen sharp pencils. But it drastically improves your chances of getting your project approved, or if you're a board member, drastically improves your confidence level when approving it. It also gives you an excuse to pat your people (and yourself!) on the back when things go according to plan. (Which is much more likely to happen, since you've done the homework!)

44. On Remembering Names

Names were not so much dropped as thrown in a perpetual game of catch.

-Robert Morley

Theodore Roosevelt, Andrew Carnegie, Steven Covey, and many others share a "gift" that contributed greatly to their success.

In politics, heavy industry, and motivational speaking; this trait has proved equally important and influential. Although each of these people is or was very intelligent and astute, this is something that anyone can do if they pay more attention to it.

They remember names.

An illustration-I went to a half-day seminar on project cost estimation, which had the potential of being about as interesting as listening to paint dry. The instructor, as introduced on the syllabus, had advanced degrees in mathematics and accounting, which did not bode well for their ability to be an engaging speaker. I was dreading it, as were a number of other participants that needed the information but were not looking forward to spending half a day learning it.

What the syllabus did NOT say was that the speaker was able to learn the names of some 40 people, from very brief introductions at the beginning of the class.

She remembered them and used them frequently in the discussion. The conversation turned lively as people felt recognized and known, and brought up their own experiences and situations into the conversation.

The speaker's reviews were excellent. Participants felt that the class was "personalized," although most of the material was directly from a manual and PowerPoint slides that had been obviously prepared in advance and used with other audiences.

The trend has been toward introducing more and more characters into our professional lives. We need to know people at more and more other companies as we develop relationships with vendors, suppliers, and clients. It's also getting harder to keep track of people within our own companies, where mergers, acquisitions, reorganizations and expansions make the cast of characters ever changing.

Being acknowledged and recognized is a basic human need that is being met less and less frequently in the workplace. Knowing a person's name means recognizing them as more than just a body filling a role or function. Identifying a person by name initiates a relationship, which involves their integrity and honor. It makes people work harder, be more honest, take more pride in their work, be more satisfied with the work they do, and stick around longer.

So, even if you're "terrible with names," there are things you can do that will help.

- Pay close attention when you're being introduced. Many people are so wrapped up in worrying about the image they present, (Is my tie straight? Is there something in my teeth? And so on.) that they forget to pay attention to the person they're being introduced to. Put yourself aside for a moment and concentrate on the other people involved.

- Say the name aloud and make sure you have the pronunciation correct.

- If the name is difficult, ask the person to spell it.

- Use the name in the conversation if an opportunity presents itself to do so.

- After you get back to your desk, (or to your car, or some other private place) write down the names of people you've met and any relevant information that will be helpful in the future. You may keep names in an address book, in your planner, on a spreadsheet on the computer, or in sophisticated "contact management" software that lets you look people up by a number of factors. Just the act of writing them down helps convert them from short to long-term memory. However you store this information, use a method that makes it easy to refer to later. Next time you go to a meeting or event, use your notebook or other system to refresh your memory about the people likely to be there.

There are very few factors that require as little effort that have such a large impact in having good rapport with people as remembering names and other key facts.

45. On Being the New Boss

Fortune favors the brave.

-Terence

In one of the old Star Wars Movie, Darth Vader steps off his shuttle into the under-construction Death Star.

Accompanied by a cadre of his personal guard, black cape billowing impressively behind him, he tells the ranking officer in charge in deep, ominous tones accented by mechanical heavy breathing:

"I'm here to put you back on schedule!"

I've been "Darth Vader" several times. Or at least, that's been my task-to take a project or job, evaluate something that's happened or even gone awry, (especially in situations where a prior manager may have left unexpectedly) and "get things back on schedule." Not an easy position to be in, especially given that you're between the company leadership that expects you to perform miracles, and the people upon whom you've been inflicted usually presume the worst!

Negotiate the Assignment

The first thing you need to do is to arrange an evaluation with the people who gave you the job. Tell them you need a few days or a couple of weeks (depending on the complexity and the urgency) to get an initial assessment of the situation, and set an appointment for that time.

Then, you roll up your sleeves.

People First.

Most people are nervous around a "new boss" or project manager, so the first order of business is to start a relaxed flow of information. They'll be relieved to find that you're not here to pin blame or criticize, you just need to get things "back on track." Concentrate on meeting the cast of characters. Have a friendly meeting (it helps to bring food) or, better yet, drop in on each of them individually and suggest going to the cafeteria for a cup of coffee, even if you don't have any specific questions for them yet.

If they're not at your location, call them and introduce yourself.

This may take some time and seem rather inefficient, but we've found that it saves an immense amount of time down the road. People are much more receptive when you establish relationships first, BEFORE you have an urgent need for information or work from them. From these informal discussions, find out as much as you can. The first things are these: Who are the decision makers and approvers? Who are the subject matter experts? Where is documentation kept? Who can you get administrative information/help from? What is the culture like-do people support each other or try to assign blame for things that have gone wrong? Armed with the "people information," everything else is much easier to get. Be careful to ask your questions from a neutral standpoint, and make sure that you never imply that anyone is at fault, especially in the initial stages of "figuring out what's going on." Remember that if you're assigned this project or this department, you may have long relationships with these folks and any trust issues you create now will haunt you later. Be sure to express appreciation for people helping you, and sympathize with their discomfort in adjusting to change.

Data Second.

Collect all of the information you can about the project, especially information regarding cost, schedule and performance. (This is classic

Project Management, but it works equally well with almost any new management job or responsibility.)

Cost-Find out how much money is allocated to this project, or department, and whether it's on track. If it's not, find out how far off it is and why.

Schedule-You may find you're behind schedule. Figure out how far behind it is, and what options exist for getting back on schedule. Do you need more staff? Different tools? Can the timeframe be moved or negotiated? Seek ideas from the staff. They usually have plenty of opinions-and many great ideas.

Performance-What is expected? How is performance measured? Is there an objective standard or is performance judged by an opinion? Whose opinion, and how is it communicated? Has the performance so far been up to par? If not, what are the deficiencies?

Some of these questions may sound accusatory if you ask them of people, so get the answers from documents if you can and just confirm them with people in an objective way. Don't show nervousness or panic about how far behind you are or how. Just document everything in a way that will be as easy as possible for your management to understand, and go to you evaluation appointment. Remember that this is NOT your problem yet; this is just a situation you're evaluating!

Evaluation Meeting

This is your opportunity to set the baseline-anything that has happened before this date is NOT your responsibility-you're merely reporting the facts. Anything that happens beyond this date IS your responsibility so be careful to lay out everything that might cause concern.

Present the facts as you've found them, on cost, schedule, and performance. Do NOT imply fault of anyone, if you can avoid it. Your job is to fix the situation, not be the attorney for the prosecution!

Also present questions that you HAVEN'T been able to find answers to, and ask for help if needed with the roadblocks and obstacles.

Present whatever options you have so far, at a high level, and let the management make their decisions and set the priorities. If the cost and risk are high enough, the company may decide to kill the project or department. If that's the case, remember NOT to defend it. You can always find another job or assignment, but you can't fix a ruined reputation from going down with a sinking ship. Remember that at this point, you're just a neutral reporter just observing the situation.

If it's decided to continue, ask for priority and direction as appropriate, and move forward. Once the decisions are made from your evaluation, you can present the priorities and direction to your team. They will probably find clear direction reassuring after what they've been through, and be happy to move forward.

Congratulations-you've just made the transition from "Darth Vader" to "manager" or "team lead" without death, destruction or undue mayhem!

46. ON ACCOUNTABILITY

Lots of folks confuse bad management with destiny.

-Kim Hubbard

I try to live what I consider a "poetic existence." That means I take responsibility for the air I breathe and the space I take up. I try to be immediate, to be totally present for all my work.

-Maya Angelou

Dear, never forget one little point: It's my business. You just work here.
-Elizabeth Arden to her husband

I believe that every right implies a responsibility; every opportunity, an obligation; every possession, a duty.

-John D. Rockefeller

Working for a living isn't what it used to be.

Being a manager, or "supervisor," was fairly simple. A "responsible" or "accountable" employee showed up each morning ten minutes early, remained quietly diligent at his workstation for 8 hours or longer, (minus the bare minimum of legally required breaks) and went home.

The "responsible" or "accountable" employee kept socializing around the water cooler to a minimum, and you knew he was working because there was nothing else to do at work-no corporate gyms, no PCs with games or the Internet to waste time on.

With technology and the unemployment rate being what it is, you may find yourself managing people who spend their time in ways that are less clear-some work at home, others may come in early or take a break during the day to use the company gym, or stay late or work weekends to make up for time taken off during the week to go to their kids' little league games and other events.

Project teams and special committees collaborate and brainstorm. To the uninformed eye, creative synergy and unproductive socializing are practically indistinguishable.

Needless to say, paying people solely based on the amount of time they spend alone in a cubicle is not a meaningful measure of their contributions to the company.

Rather than relying on a managers and supervisors to walk the halls and ensure that everyone is present and accounted for, and "looking busy," management has evolved to the art of setting appropriate objectives (or participating with workgroups in setting their objectives) encouraging an atmosphere that rewards accountability, and measuring and rewarding performance that directly relates to the company's bottom line.

This includes:

- Educating people on the company's mission and objectives.
- Ensuring each person understands how his job affects everyone else's.
- Demonstrating good examples of appropriate contributions.
- Encouraging and rewarding creative solutions, as long as the results meet requirements and expectations.
- Being as flexible as possible with the work environment as long as company objectives are met.
- Respecting and trusting each individual to manage his or her own time as much as possible within the parameters of the job.
- Ensuring accountability by measuring and communicating performance results.
- Even if you pay by the hour, financial incentives should be tied to those performance measures.

In a way, management hasn't changed much from what it's always been-ensuring that work gets done.

In other ways, it's light years easier, and more difficult; depending on your ability to be resourceful and to accept change.

47. ON TRAINING

Creative minds have always been known to survive any kind of bad training.

-Anna Freud

The secret in education lies in respecting the student.

-Ralph Waldo Emerson

How much money did your company spend on training last year? And of that, how much of it was actually relevant and useful?

Many companies are finding themselves with a workforce that is exceptionally well-"trained" on specific tools and processes, but also under-"educated" in the sense that these same employees don't understand the relevance of these tools to their everyday jobs, how they affect their own performance, or relate to the company's performance.

According to CIO magazine, the first problem is that word: training. It conjures up images of dogs jumping through hoops. This is not helpful. "I separate training into two parts-education and training," says John Conklin, vice president and CIO of World Kitchen (formerly Corning Consumer Products Co., manufacturer of Pyrex and Corningware) of Elmira, N.Y. "Education is all the why, who and where issues," Conklin says. "Training is the how part of the equation." And of the two, he says, "education is the bigger piece of the puzzle. If people don't go through this education, you won't have their hearts and you won't have their minds."

There's a tendency for companies to fall into the trap of putting employees through training programs that are too software-specific-an easy mistake to make, since it's so easy to hire a software vendor to complete the training when you buy a software package.

There are many firms that offer generic tools-based training, and very few that will actually understand your business well enough to translate that for students into "when, where and why" training rather than just the "how" of how to use a specific tool. You have lots of employees that know intimately what this button does and what that field is for, in a specific software program, for example. But they may not know what happens to that information after it's entered and what impact an error or incomplete entry would have on their coworkers or on the customer's order.

It's like being an expert electrician, but not understanding whether you're wiring a home or a factory.

People have to understand the nature of the business, and how the products of their work are going to be used by their co-workers, and ultimately, by the customer. That way, the electrician can use his skills to spend the time and money allocated to his part of the project in ways that really benefits the family that lives in the house, or the business that works in the factory.

When the annual budget process begins each year, you may want to evaluate spending on training. Revising your training programs to be less tools-specific and more business-relevant usually requires more time from your own people, and more judicious spending on "prepackaged" training programs from software vendors or generic training-providers. It doesn't have to cost more, but it does require a bit more planning.

The rewards of a more holistic educational approach are a workforce that is not only fluent in the use of software packages, but also more fluent in how to leverage those tools for the benefit of your company and your customers.

48. On Asking Questions

The mere formulation of a problem is far more often essential than its solution, which may be merely a matter of mathematical or experiment skill.

-Albert Einstein

Good questions outrank easy answers.

-Paul A. Samuelson

Most managers spend too much time talking. They have the misconception that a good manager has all the answers.

Look around your average meeting, and you see the top dog expounding values, espousing ideas, explaining strategy, and urging his subjects to greater performance. Everyone else is doodling on their notepad, putting on his best "attentive" face, stirring her coffee, or contemplating the state of the universe. There's usually nothing wrong with the content of what's being communicated.

Unfortunately, EVERYTHING is wrong with the WAY it's being communicated. Ninety percent of the contents of the meeting will be forgotten upon leaving the room. One hundred percent of the people, including the boss, are already dreading the next meeting.

How can you avoid this apathy? One way is to spend less time using declarative sentences and more time asking questions. Socrates, the ancient Greek who is known as the father of philosophy, taught his students by asking questions. Many excellent teachers, and managers, employ the same methods.

Common questions:

- How do you think we should solve this problem?
- Who has run into a situation like this before?
- What did you do about it? Did it work? What would you do differently?
- What would you suggest?

Many good managers I know will keep their opinions to themselves, even if they have a pretty good idea of how to solve a problem. They'll let a team member come up with the idea and own it, even if it's a variation that doesn't quite match up with what the manager has in mind. Although this may seem like a waste of time, it usually more than makes up for the extra time by improving morale, encouraging buy-in and accountability among team members, and takes it off your plate so you can devote your time and energy to other things.

If asking questions hasn't been your style, you may find yourself facing deafening silence the first time or two you pose a question in a meeting. People may be shy about coming forward, they may be unused to offering their ideas, and/or they may not even be awake. These are all good reasons to change the format of your meetings. Unfortunately, many managers take silence for ambivalence or incompetence, and jump to the conclusion "The Socratic style is interesting, but it doesn't work in this environment or with these people."

This reticence can be overcome. Here are some ideas-

- Be encouraging. "I know you guys know this stuff. I've seen what you can do."
- Be positive. Redirect ideas without being critical. Rather than saying "That won't work." Try something more like-"That's a good idea, but did you consider…."
- Be persistent. Commit to trying this style for at least three consecutive meetings before making a judgment-people may be

unprepared at first and will take some time to expect the questions and come prepared to answer them. Don't let them off the hook and supply your own ideas too soon.

- Be proactive. Provide resources and reference materials, and publish agendas in advance so that people have the opportunity to "come up to speed" before the meeting.

- Be rewarding. Publicly thank (or reward) people who come up with good ideas or implement good solutions. Show how it contributed to the bottom line or made other employee's lives easier.

- Include the right people. Don't ask programming questions of customer service reps, or ask user questions of programmers. If you can get a mixed group to participate, you have the best chance of coming out with "rounded," really useful ideas.

- Document the outcome. This helps everyone remember what happened, what was committed to, acknowledge the individuals who offered ideas, and validates the contributions of everyone who participated. Everyone loves to see his name in print, (or at least pays attention) even when it's next to an action item.

People may never love meetings, but may find they look forward to the opportunity to present their ideas, participate with their team members, and play a more active role in contributing to the company's success.

49. On Mistakes

Freedom is not worth having if it does not include the freedom to make mistakes.

-Mahatma Gandhi

A computer lets you make more mistakes faster than any invention in human history—with the possible exceptions of handguns and tequila.

-Mitch Ratliffe

If everything appears to be going well, you don't know what the hell is going on.

-Anonymous

Life is a work in progress. If we all knew perfectly what we were doing, we probably wouldn't be on this planet-we would have graduated to some perfect existence where decisions are all foregone conclusions and there are no messy implications, emergencies or loose ends.

Many executives suffer from "analysis paralysis"-an illness characterized by fear of making a decision because it may be in error. In many cases, even making a wrong decision is better than making no decision. One company may make a wrong decision, learn from it and correct it in the amount of time another company may spend in endless deliberation and red tape. A company that suffers from "analysis paralysis" has a chilling effect on new ideas, demoralizes its more creative employees, and also suffers from a lack momentum and inertia.

To prevent that, companies can find ways to minimize the effects of errors on their customers without unacceptably slowing themselves down.

- Microsoft releases software with the assumption that they will find bugs. For each release of major software (such as their operating systems or Office suites) they release several "service packs" to software purchasers that correct errors or shore up weaknesses. They know that if they wait until the software is perfect to get it to market, their competition would have time to develop their own products first and they would lose potential buyers.

- Having an acceptable level of risk does not excuse producing a shoddy product or providing inferior service. All great companies strive for higher quality and fewer mistakes.

- The difference is that great companies balance the drive for quality with a creative, adventurous spirit that takes risks (and potentially makes mistakes.)

- How do you hit the right balance?

- Create "error-traps." An example-I read a notice on a can of Oregon cherries-"We want your pits!" They advise consumers to send in pits and pit fragments, along with the code from the bottom of the can. Consumers then receive a certificate for a free can of Oregon fruit. This is a great way of admitting to the possibility that the pitting and canning process may not be perfect, and allows customers to feel like they have some recourse. It also gives Oregon information to improve their processes and equipment by being informed of errors.

- Use a "throwaway" draft or model when planning something new, with the understanding that there will be mistakes. Include lots of people in the critiquing phase. Reward people for finding mistakes or errors in your work, rather than getting defensive or punitive.

- Create a "beta process." Allow some of your customer volunteers to participate in your evaluation of a new product or services by publicizing it as a "beta" or new release and spending the time to understand how it meets (or doesn't meet) the customer's needs. This gives the customers some extra attention, and gives you information you need to correct mistakes, or prevent the launch of a product that is truly flawed.

- Never cover up a mistake. Consumers, clients, partners and vendors are always much more understanding of an honest mistake than they are of a cover-up. Admit it freely, make the effort to ensure that impacts are mitigated, and keep the communications open.

These are simple things you can do to avoid "analysis paralysis" by making it safer to take risks, make mistakes and learn from them.

50. ON REINVENTING THE WHEEL

Many companies are constantly reinventing the wheel.

How many different phone lists does your company have? If you include customer databases, direct mail systems, the contact management files of each individual salesperson, the vendor management information from each manager, employee contact lists, payroll and human resources information? Could this information come from a single source if it were possible to allow different levels of access and customize lists on demand?

Does each of your customer representatives write a letter from scratch whenever they need to contact a customer regarding a problem? Are many of problems common among a variety of customers? You may find many of your people keep files of "good letters" to reuse when they need to; but are they sharing them with each other?

You may find that each employee develops his own "secrets of success" to make his or her job easier. He probably spends a great deal of time maintaining his own contact information, keeping successful documents, and developing his own "best practices." Often these "secrets" are jealously guarded, especially in a competitive environment, such as a sales department where everybody keeps develops his or her own leads and doesn't want a co-worker to profit from his hard work. But many times, these things are not shared for other reasons-

- Not knowing that anyone else would find it useful.
- Not having a vehicle to share common practices.
- Fearing criticism from revealing ones' methods.
- Incentives and rewards are placed on individual performance rather than group contributions.

By keeping tools and resources isolated, your company spends exponentially more effort than needed by keeping (and constantly updating) independent kingdoms of tools and information.

New employees will find your company bewildering and take a long time to "learn the ropes." You'll suffer lots of downtime if someone quits or goes on vacation because "She was the only person who knew how to do this."

How can you promote resource sharing?

Parameters

It is NOT appropriate to encourage vital resource sharing in an environment that is competitive out of necessity. For example, real estate professionals and commissioned salespeople should not be asked to share their hard-earned lead information, because that is compromising their ability to make money from their efforts. It MAY be appropriate, however, to ask them to share some marketing and correspondence information that has helped them to be successful. You will need to tailor the level of interdependence based on the nature of your business and the degree of cooperation your employees already enjoy.

Develop a "Knowledge Pool"

Provide a vehicle to capture best practices when you find them. This could be as simple as a loose-leaf notebook for outstanding letters and correspondence, which is open to the entire staff to borrow and use for their own letters. It could be as complicated as an online "resource library" which makes documents, templates, databases, spreadsheets, and calculators accessible to everyone using the company's Intranet.

By publicizing the availability of a best-practices sharing vehicle, people may become more aware that the things they do and use every day may be of wider use (and greater value) than they think!

Syndication

You will invariably run across instances where two or more tools, spreadsheets or letters serve the same function, and each will have some advantages over the other. Two contact lists, for example, may surface-each of which is slightly better than the other for a certain purpose. Should you continue to support the ongoing maintenance of both lists? Maybe you could have the owners of both lists get together (with a facilitator or other interested parties if necessary) and brainstorm possible improvements that would define synergies between the lists and/or leverage a common process to update both.

Concentrate on the positive qualities of both tools, ensuring that both parties "get credit" for their contributions, but make it clear that they will be even better if they can be held in common by the company.

Incentives

You may need to provide incentives for people to participate in knowledge sharing, especially if your environment has typically rewarded individual performance over teamwork. Here are a few ideas:

Each time someone contributes something useful to the "knowledge pool," his or her name is added to a drawing for a prize.

- Have employees vote for the best contribution or most-used tool.

- Offer a small prize or recognition for each contribution.

- Use contributions to the "knowledge pool" as criteria for performance evaluations.

- Set an expectation of teamwork and cooperation. Seed the "knowledge pool" with your own contributions.

- Promote awareness and use of the "knowledge pool" whenever an opportunity presents itself. Whenever an employee seeks advice about the task, coach them to make it a habit to research the "knowledge pool" before developing any list or spreadsheet that might possibly already exist. "Check first, invent second."

If you have a "knowledge pool" containing a variety of "wheels," new employees will come up to speed faster. Existing employees may find new ways of doing things. People will be recognized and rewarded for finding creative ways to share information, or improve existing information. And you'll be able to devote more time and money to pursuing your objectives, rather than reinventing wheels.

ABOUT THE AUTHOR

Paula Gamonal is a manager in the financial industry. She founded Ravenwerks in 1997 with a few dedicated cohorts, and has since worked on web sites, technology projects and other consulting work for various businesses. She has a Bachelor of Arts in Communications from the University of Utah, and is contemplating their EMBA program. She has a black belt in the martial art of Tae Kwon Do, and lives in Tooele, Utah.

www.ingramcontent.com/pod-product-compliance
Lightning Source LLC
Chambersburg PA
CBHW030742180526
45163CB00003B/895